SAINT MARGARET OF CORTONA

Saint Margaret of
Cortona

BY

FRANÇOIS MAURIAC

TRANSLATED FROM THE FRENCH
BY BERNARD FRECHTMAN

Lord, Thou hast struck my heart with
Thy words and I have loved Thee.

Saint Augustine
"Confessions," x, 6

PHILOSOPHICAL LIBRARY

New York

Preface

SAINT MARGARET OF CORTONA, SHE WHO HAS become so dear to me to-day, did not obtrude herself upon me. I had no wish to write a saint's life, especially hers, which I knew nothing about. I had no desire to write anything. The whole earth was covered with darkness. Was it in '41, in '42, in '43? Time no longer seemed divided; all of those winters formed nothing more than a black and frozen block in our minds. We lived them at Malagar in the womb of a monotonous horror. There was a German in every room. An enemy accordion groaned near the kitchen. Whether it was sunny or whether the rain streamed against the panes, the landscape was hopeless.

All the same, it was necessary to write. One could not live on air only, nor on the outrages of a press that was drunk with rage. A Jesuit Father from Lyons claimed that it was I who was responsible for losing the war and that the reading of my novels had deterred French youth from fighting. In M. Henri Bordeaux's *The Walls Are Good* literature had, if I may say so, a good strong shoulder to lean on.

To write—but what to write? The publisher of *The Life of Jesus,* faithful to the discredited author I then was, looked to me for the biography of a saint. I yielded to his friendly insistence. Still, it was necessary to make a choice among so many blessed ones. The greatest have served so very much.

Margaret of Cortona aroused my interest because she is very little known in France. I knew that she had first succumbed to the most human kind of love and that she had even had a child ("That's just the one for you!") What finally decided me was that the essential material concerning her is contained in a book written by her confessor, one to which the most learned can add hardly anything.

Well, circumstances prohibited me from travelling, from research in libraries (which, moreover, I would not have done in any case, even if there had not been an occupation or a war). By the same token, I was able to dispense with having to paint the historical setting in which our saint was steeped and was obliged to follow my own taste, which was to limit myself strictly to the history of a soul. As the external events of this life amount to hardly anything, my book has become a kind of meditation on mystical states, in which I yield, by turns, to the attraction and the irritation which they inspire in me.

What is also expressed there, especially in the last chapters, are the moments of despair which we were then going through. Margaret of Cortona drew me out of this abominable world. I followed this poor woman as far as it pleased her to lead me; I understood her love; I entered fully into her being. I heard what she had heard. I extracted what was essential, despite the distortions of her confessor and of those who later touched up his work. But also I was sometimes angry with myself for writing an untimely book at this point. The martyrdom of the woman from Cortona distracted me from the martyrdom of my country; it made me unfaithful to that blood-soaked earth. It seems to me that the eddyings of my heart and thoughts around this forgotten thirteenth century saint give a peculiar accent to this book. It should be borne in mind, while reading, that such and such a chapter was interrupted because it was the hour of the "Frenchmen Speak to Frenchmen" radio program or because heavy boots were shaking the ceiling or because the fanfares of the great German Master-state were announcing over the radio a Reich victory.

Later, I returned to Paris to take shelter and to work with the underground press. But those dark days before the Resistance, in the heart of a countryside flooded with rain, wasted by the sun, where, beyond all endurance, I was more bored than at any other time in my life, are incarnated for me in this passionate little saint who was bent on destroying a face that was so beautiful that after years of fierce penance it still frightened the brothers of the monastery of Cortona. Perhaps it will frighten and even horrify some of those who will read my book, for Margaret is not a saint for the men of to-day who stray so far from the light.

A saint for the men of to-day. . . . I sometimes try to imagine this creature suddenly risen

up, and once again making Christ sensible to
the heart of a mankind blinded with blood,
driven out of all its places of refuge—even
from the materialistic prison where it has been
sheltering itself for nearly two centuries—and
spiritually hemmed in.

Will he be a workingman, a member of the
Young Catholic Workers, a suburban vicar? A
humble man, in any case, through whom grace
will blaze forth powerfully and gloriously to the
beholder. "This generation asks for a sign."
Yes, and it asks from the depth of such an
abyss, with an urgency so shot through with
despair that we can no longer doubt that it is approaching—that hour when the Love we have
believed in will manifest itself at last.

F. M.

Paris

Contents

CHAPTER I

Too Young and Too Pretty

ONE DAY IN THE YEAR 1273 A WOMAN IN mourning, holding a little boy by the hand, knocked at the door of the Franciscan convent of the Celle, two and a half miles from Cortona. She must have walked a long time to get to this wild gorge hollowed out in Mount Sant-Egidio where a torrent almost spatters the cells of the Minorites with its spray.

The porter was moved on seeing this exhausted woman whose gold and pearl chains were perhaps still binding her hair. He went off in a hurry to get the superior. The unknown woman asked not for alms but the garb of penitence. The first tears of repentance added to her eyes a grace which could not escape the Brother Superior, despite a short, quickly averted look, for he dismissed her with a very

1

gentle word (but it was to weigh heavily on the
destiny of this Margaret), "My daughter, you
are too young and too pretty."

Too pretty. . . . It was doubtless on the
route which led her to Cortona that Margaret
began to hate that too charming body. Because
of the errors into which it had led her, it was
already her enemy; and now her charm even
kept her from approaching the sanctuary, and
her appearance alone made holy people flee her.
Ah! this impure beauty which raised itself between her desire and her God. Meanwhile, the
little boy was crying and nagging her with questions: "Will we be there soon? I'm thirsty . . .
my feet hurt." But she wasn't listening to him,
almost indifferent, already completely turned to
the side of her new love, her eternal love!

Margaret hastened on, assured of being led
she knew not where, but there where her God
wanted her. However, with the furious hatred
of her body, the terror of not being able to be
saved grew in her heart after the repulse which
she suffered at the Celle, a terror which would
end only with her life, despite the signal grace

with which she was to be loaded and over-whelmed.

She entered Cortona by the Berarda gate. Two women who were passing by stopped. The elder was named Marinaria Moscari; the younger was her daughter-in-law Renaria. They hesitated a few seconds before addressing this stranger. But, accustomed as they were to works of mercy, they had doubtless learned not to be taken in; at the first glance, they recognized one of those wretches who are not simply being dramatic. Perhaps they also yielded to the charm of the weeping face. Two Minorites had fled before such a formidable beauty but the Moscari women did not have the same reasons to be frightened; and who in Italy does not have a passion for handsome faces?

Margaret answered them with complete confidence; but in the street she had only to tell the merest bit necessary to arouse the curiosity of the holy women and to bring to the highest pitch that hunger for souls, that need to lay hands on all those who passed by their door, with which Marinaria in particular seems to have been possessed. The confession continued and concluded in one of the rooms of the Moscari house, and its effect was such that the women would no longer allow the child or the mother to set out again.

CHAPTER II

The Delicious and Criminal Way of the World

OF HER FIRST YEARS IN LAVIANO, AN UMBRIAN village not far from Lake Trasimene, in the fever-ridden vale of Chiana, where Margaret was born in 1247, we know hardly anything. Perhaps her father was a tenant of the Municipio of Perugia; he was only a poor farmer. Her mother, who had given her the taste for prayer, died when Margaret was seven years old. Two years later her father remarried, and from the very beginning there was warfare between the child and the new wife.

Adolescents who are despised in the family circle become dangerously sensitive to the love that they inspire on the outside. Hardly did she cross the threshold of the house, the house where she knew she was hated, where her very beauty, far from winning to her the hearts of others, made her stepmother more jealous, when the reign of Margaret began.

She knew the intoxication of those first conquests which give reassurance as a humiliated childhood draws to a close. So we are not this monster after all, this object of family derision! Margaret became aware of her charm, her power. Peasant that she was, she even enchanted the manor lords, and even the chief of them all, that gentleman from Montepulciano, the lord, it may be, of Laviano and the Villa Palazzi.

All biographers of the saint have tried hard to make this young man out to be a seducer who won her with gifts, deceived her by a promise of marriage and kept her almost by force for nine years . . . which does not keep the saint's first biographer, Brother Giunta Bevegnati, from showing us a triumphant Margaret "in luxurious garments, her hair adorned with gold chains, going out only on horseback or in a carriage, her face painted, proud of her lover's wealth."

Was she married? Everything leads us to believe that she was not. The testimony of Bevegnati is explicit on this point. But then, under what title did she reign during those nine years at the castle of Montepulciano? Wadding (in the *Annals of the Minorites,* volume V) insinuates that she had affairs. The only thing we can be quite sure of is this: she lived in evil, "in crime and in dishonor." She did evil; and she did it in the presence of One Who had already chosen her, had already marked her with His sign. What the story of Margaret teaches us is that a creature may, at the very depths of her wretchedness, be already elected. We are not dealing with a matter of conjecture. We know only very little about her guilty life, but this little comes from a source which does not deceive. After a certain moment, Christ spoke to her, and most of the circumstances of her life are known to us only because the Lord recalled them to His *poor daughter,* to His *poor little one* as He called her.

Thus, we would have been forever ignorant of the fact that on the night of her abduction, when she had to make her way with her seducer over the twelve miles which separated her from Montepulciano, they barely escaped perishing in the swamps of the Chiana, had not the Lord himself spoken to her about it: "My poor daughter, remember the crossing of that pond, alone, in the middle of the night, when the ancient enemy wanted to drown you with your accomplice at the moment when you were getting ready by your crimes to renew the agony of My Passion; but My divine clemency has preserved you, and you have been delivered by an infinite mercy."

The inner words that mystics believe they have heard are not transmitted to us quite purely. There is hardly a one which does not offer itself to us without some lingering doubt, because they lack the bareness of those that the synoptics have preserved for us, where the very accent of the Lord is still perceptible. In the greatest souls, the inner words make their way through an impoverished nature still pervaded by passions of a mediocre sort.

It is enough to read the book called *Divine Words,* in which Father Saudreau has collected a part of what holy souls throughout the cen-

turies have heard within themselves, to see to
what extent the ridiculously human is sometimes mixed in. It happens that a vein of silli-
ness gets into them, to the point that the au-
thentic part of the Lord is hardly discernible
there any longer.

However, what was addressed to two Italian sinners of the thirteenth century, Saint
Angela of Foligno and our Margaret of Cortona, has a particular ring there, as if human
love had destroyed in them what blameless lives
are sometimes encumbered with. Here nothing
remains but the ash and the burned rock and
the exquisite voice which bursts forth above a
desert where all vegetation has been consumed
by fire.

Human genius alone (on one of the rare
occasions when it has heard and collected the
words of Christ) has been able to pipe off the
divine water, almost unmixed, at its source. I
am thinking of *Pascal's Mystery of Jesus* which
Father Saudreau has taken care not to include
in his collection. Perhaps this is right, because
in this case we have only a layman who only
yesterday was still entangled in the world, at-

tached to a theology that is suspect, a very mass
of imperfections and miseries, so that the word
reaches us directly, not yet deformed, nor chan-
nelized, nor submitted to any censorship.

The same does not go for the message of
Margaret of Cortona which her confessor has
carefully filtered. Abbé Brémond speaks some-
where of the fatal transformation that the
words of a mystic may undergo when reported
by a prejudiced director. Very often the voice
of the good Brother Giunta Bevegnati covers
another voice or muddies it, weighs it down
with human properties. (And I am not taking
into account all the errors of editing, transcrip-
tion, and translation.) Therefore, we shall have
to penetrate through the commentator and try
to overhear the word that Margaret herself
heard when her heart was one with God's—
with that God of Whom it seems one can say
nothing that is not a lie, but to Whom it is
vouchsafed us to speak and to Whom it is possible to listen when He addresses Himself, not
to our unworthy selves, but to His preferred
ones.

CHAPTER III

The Preferred Sinner

HIS PREFERRED ONE. . . . AT MONTEPULCIANO,
Margaret the sinner was already such. Everything came about from this choice made in the
midst of crime. Her crucified life was in embryo
during her nine years of forbidden pleasures.
Sin, her sin, did not for a moment divert the
loving attention of Him who had chosen and
had brooded over her from all eternity. "Remember that while you were enjoying yourself
in the world and were leading a life full of
darkness, vice, and sin, I made myself your
master, your guide, and inspired you with
genuine compassion for the poor and the afflicted. I made you taste, then, so great a joy
of solitude that in a rush of devotion, you cried
out, 'Oh! how good it would be here to taste the
delights of prayer. Oh! how well the praises of
God should be sung here! With what security,

11

with what peace might one pass his days here in penitence!' Remember that, despite the darkness which enveloped your soul, you deplored your fall, and you told those who greeted you that if they knew about your shameful life, not only would they not greet you but they would not even want to talk to you."

On the eve of her death, little Thérèse of Lisieux announced to her Sisters the earthly glory that was going to crown her holiness. She knew that, at the same time that she had conquered heaven, she had also conquered the world. This certainty seems more astonishing in a lost woman such as the sinner of Montepulciano was. "What will become of you, proud Margaret?" her jealous companions asked her; and they predicted a disgraceful old age for her. But the kept woman, instead of lowering her head, defied them: "A time will come when you will call me a saint, and you will go on a pilgrimage to my tomb with the staff and wallet of the pilgrim."

This destiny of glory, which a little martyred Carmelite had discovered, as from the height of the cross, on the sick-bed where she had consummated her suffering, Margaret, who had a lover and who had brought a child of sin into the world, saw coming from the depth of her shame, and gloried in it with a mysterious assurance.

Sinners, convinced that no possible communication exists between the Creator and His defiled creature, do not know that lost grace does not mean that God's love has been lost, that there is a confrontation of our soul with God that no crime can interrupt, to which, on the contrary, sin adds an element of drama, for it accentuates that which distinguishes us from others, that which singles us out among all others for redeeming love, as if a certain way of opposing ourselves to God were only an unconscious ruse to impose ourselves upon Him.

Margaret was to expiate the delights which enchanted her and she already knew that she would expiate them. But first she had to go through the moments of crime to attain the moments of restoration and in order for her whole life to be ordered, to be composed according to a model already offered to humanity thirteen centuries earlier—this woman whose hair was unbound and whose vase was filled with a very precious perfume.

To say that God is there, whatever we may do, is not to reduce the gravity of our failings; it is rather to put us on guard against that facility of no longer paying attention to the divine, indestructible presence within us with the pretext of lost grace. What Christian, in his bad hours, has not had the cowardly experience of this ignoble euphoria: "At last He's no longer there! You may indulge yourself to your heart's content." But He is always there, and Margaret, at Montepulciano, knew that sin does not deliver us from this eternal witness.

Her life had been shameful. He Himself reminded her of that, He Who, despite this shame, had not screened His face from her. All she *remembers* that Christ tirelessly repeated to her constrained the penitent not to lose sight of that obstinate presence of God at the very center of her shame, as present in the life of the sinner as it can be absent from the life of a Pharisee.

For Margaret nothing remained but faith.

"I had lost honor," she must have written after her conversion, "dignity, peace, everything, except faith." She awaited the blow, not knowing from what side she would be struck. We can not doubt the fact that Margaret was a woman who had been loved, since it was in her lover that she was struck. Perhaps she had believed that the debate concerned her alone and that on the day of vengeance there could be no other victim than herself. But the man who separated her from God had been spied upon for nine years, awaited at a turning point of his life by that rival Who is not seen.

CHAPTER IV

The Lover Murdered

AT THE BEGINNING OF THE YEAR 1273 THE young lord, accompanied by Margaret, left Montepulciano for Villa Palazzi either because he wanted to visit his estate or because he had to settle some difference with a neighboring landowner. According to a tradition which has no basis in any of the old texts (it is only through an utterance of Christ that we know that Margaret's accomplice came to a tragic end,) he set out alone one morning, followed by a favorite dog. Two days later the greyhound returned without its master. It moaned, licked Margaret's hand, and pulled her by the dress. In this way she was led to the foot of an oak in the forest of Petrignano, about a mile from Pozzuolo. There the dog redoubled his moans. Margaret pushed aside the freshly cut branches and discovered the corpse, pierced by stabs, already decomposed.

And forthwith she saw the Other, she found herself face to face with that Other Who, at no moment, had ever turned away from her, Who, during the woman's worst abasements, had not veiled His face, but Who on the contrary, had never stopped looking at her.

Confronted with these terrible remains, with this rotted flesh, the young woman suffered, but already felt herself saved. This corruption was like something torn out of her, torn out of her bowels.

If Margaret had loved the unfortunate man with all her soul as she had cherished him with her whole body, doubtless she would have mastered her despair in order to get someone to avenge him. But it does not seem that she went to a moment's trouble to discover the murderers. The real Author of this murder—she knew Him; He was there; He had always been there. What did it matter to her that her lover had slipped off to "eternal infidelity," as Chateaubriand calls the death of lovers. She too, at the same moment, had resolved to be eternally unfaithful to him and gave herself forever to Him Who had separated them.

The Abbé de Rancé has written that "those who die well or badly more often die for those whom they have left behind in the world than for themselves." Whether the family of the murdered man would have cast her off or not, Margaret's break with the world was immediate, total, in front of that rotting body half covered with branches, beneath the oak which had been the witness of the crime.

And yet, she who had faith could not doubt that her accomplice, at that very hour, had been judged and had received his due.

Now, Margaret, who, in her dialogues with the Saviour, often pleaded for assurances concerning the salvation of her parents, her son, her director, was never to mention the unknown and hitherto adored name. Had she known the fate of that guilty soul—a fact which would explain the terror which never ceased to pervade her love for Christ? Had the jealous God made her hear, from beyond the shore of the dead and from the very first moment, the cry of horror of him who had been her idol in this world?

Unless He had kept His penitent in doubt, leaving the door of hope partly open: "With men this is impossible: but with God all things are possible." It is the most consoling saying of Christ in the Gospel, one which answers an almost desperate question: "Who then can be saved?" Everything is possible to God, even opening heaven to a young idiot brusquely assaulted and killed in the corruption of his adolescence.

Margaret saved herself without turning her head, returned to the Villa, got rid of all her jewels, and took her child by the hand.

CHAPTER V

Under Nathanael's Fig-Tree

SHE FOLLOWED THE CONQUEROR. SHE GAVE herself to the stronger. She had to return to the point from which she had fled at the hour of her sin. Her place was at Laviano, in the house of her father, despite that unimaginable torment, her step-mother's triumphant hatred, and that scorn which would be distilled for her hour by hour. But something that she had not foreseen happened to her. Despite the protests of her unnerved and cowardly father, the old woman cried out that she would leave the house the day that scandalous daughter put her foot in it. And she shut the door on Margaret.

So the worst ordeal that Margaret had imagined was avoided. It was not permitted her to weigh her courage against the anguish to which she had acquiesced in advance. And she once again found herself alone with her little boy in the garden where she had been an unhappy child, a girl who had been tempted. It was here that, like another Margaret, she had gazed in secret on those jewels that an Umbrian Faust had chosen. He had prowled about these walls; perhaps he had climbed over them. He Who now held her demanded a final victory over this murdered rival who, since she remembered him, was still alive in her.

One evening she had left this garden. She had run toward the boat in which she would have been carried away if the invisible God had not kept guard at the stern. But though she might have escaped from the phantoms of her love, there remained that hatred reawakened by the step-mother who had insulted her, who had chased her from her father's house and cast her out into the darkness.

Only yesterday, at Montepulciano, she had triumphed again. Despite the murder of her lover, what had she lost of that which had made her queen? She was twenty-six years old and knew the power of her radiant beauty. Had she not accomplished all that lay in her power?

Was it her fault if her father disowned
her?

Not knowing what decision to make, Margaret had sat down beneath the fig-tree in the
garden; and we muse on the mysterious words
of the Lord to Nathanael: "Before that Philip
called, thee, when thou wast under the fig tree,
I saw thee" (John 1:48). Margaret too. Jesus
had seen her, an innocent little thing, playing in
the shade of the old tree, while she foresaw
nothing of her approaching shame nor of her
distant glory; and later He had seen her, her
heart full of anxiety, perhaps on the look-out
or re-reading a message whose every word
burned her. . . . And now He was seeing her
again, trembling; but she had already chosen;
here she was, completely surrendered, delivered
up, although a voice whispered to her, "Go
back to your pleasure, you are beautiful, you
shall have lovers to defend you, you whose
parents have chased you out."

But Margaret was already won over to
other pleasures. "Remember, *ma poveretta,*"
the Lord must have said to her at a later time,
"how you returned to Laviano, near your

father, after the tragic death of your accomplice, bathed in tears, crushed, annihilated with
grief, your face lacerated, dressed in mourning. . . . Remember how boorishly your father
received you at your stepmother's instigation.
. . . Not knowing where to go, without advice
or help, seated under the fig-tree in the garden,
you humbly implored and asked Me to be henceforth your master, father, spouse, and lord.
Then the old serpent seized this opportunity to
persuade you that your beautiful body, your
fresh youth, and this humiliating exile were
reasons enough to throw you into crime. And
he hinted that wherever you went you would
find accomplices and worshippers. But I, Who
reform all inner beauty, charmed with that
beauty you had just profaned, inspired you to
make your way to Cortona and submit yourself
to My Minorites."

She got up, went away from the garden forever, still dragging her little boy, and took the
route to Cortona. This inner beauty with which
her God had been charmed would once again
be resplendent when the other fatal beauty
which had pushed her into crime would be anni-

hilated once and for all. Here she was, her
mind already made up for this annihilation. A
woman's struggle unto death against her weak
flesh, almost the whole subject of this story,
horrifies our reason. But Margaret was no
longer subjected to the domination of reason.
She was a sinner who no longer knew anything
but her sin and her love, who no longer had eyes
for anything outside of what this love required.
To wither her beauty, to become her own execu-
tioner in order to satisfy the demand of a crucified God, could she imagine anything more
unreasonable? But she scorned the fact that
her behavior ran the risk of appearing mad to
the rest of the world. She meditated on what
she knew to be true. For her, the truth which
exceeded all evidence was that she had to
humble that voluptuous body which separated
her from her Lord, Who had been crowned with
thorns, Whose hands and feet had been pierced,
Whose side had been torn open. For Margaret,
the truth was that she had to start this task immediately, at that very moment of her life,
while she was still drawing breath, and she
hastened along the route to Cortona, dragging

her weakened child by the hand, the child of her sin, already promised to the funeral-pile of Isaac.

Concerning this particular point, her behavior would be scandalous to the world and, perhaps, to us, as was Christ's, and as His cross would be if our eye considered it, no longer gilded, radiant, and triumphant, but in its abject reality, small, low, impregnated with blood.

Margaret no longer owned anything of her own except that thorn in her flesh: what she had done every moment of her delicious and guilty youth, what she could not have helped doing, and that anguish which stifled her, and her God Who was there and Who was able to cure her.

CHAPTER VI

Margaret's Stages

THE MOSCARI WOMEN TOOK THIS MAGDALENE and her child into their house and introduced her to Brother Rinaldo of Castiglione, the warden of Arezzo, on whom the convent of Cortona was dependent. The penitent was entrusted to the care of Brother Giunta Bevegnati.

But this whole matter was not to go off without great difficulties. That too beautiful face which had made the porter and the superior of the Celle flee also frightened the Cortonian Minorites. Although Margaret, from the very first days, had declared systematic war on her body and though her penitence had already astonished the city, they did not believe that so beautiful a creature could keep this up for long nor remain out of the world. That flesh of hers, deprived of food, tortured by the hair-cloth and the lash, to which Margaret kept repeating "Thou hast conquered me, I shall conquer thee!" did not disarm their mistrust.

Brother Giunta Bevegnati confessed that he made her wait several years for the joy of donning the garb of the Third Order of the Franciscans. The mania of destruction which Margaret turned against herself was fortified by the resistance which her beauty exacted from her, a beauty upon which she never ceased inflicting the worst possible treatment.

If the Brothers had differed any longer about taking her into the Third Order what would this woman with the shaven head, dressed in tatters, her face smeared with sweat, who, disfigured in this way, still seemed terrible to them, what would she not have finally inflicted on that poor body? But, moreover, even after she had received (doubtless in 1276) the garb from the hands of Brother Rinaldo of Castiglione, she put no restraint upon that holy hatred—some of whose deeds make us shudder —which had already made her a sick woman, almost an invalid.

Dressed in the garb which she had desired so much, Margaret began another stage no less frightful than the first. But henceforth her life would be entirely a cry of love, a call between two ecstasies, for her Lord and her God were going to speak to her almost daily, and the whole city of Cortona would be intent upon this fiery dialogue.

Up to that time she had lived in seclusion among her proctresses, and in order not to be a burden on them, she took care of women in confinement and sponsored their children at baptism. In 1277 she obtained a more secluded cell from the Moscari women, outside of, but near their house, perhaps on the very spot where the Delle Poverelle monastery has been erected. It was in that year that, while praying before a crucifix venerated in the church of the Minorites and which today is in Saint Margaret's church at Cortona, she heard the Lord for the first time. "What dost thou want, my poor little one (*paupercula*)?" Margaret replied at once, "I seek nothing, I want only you."

As Brother Giunta has not followed a chronological order and never gives an exact

date (though he always indicates the Saint's
day) and relates the same episode many times,
we shall, before going further, try to set up
some guideposts. From 1277 to 1286 Margaret
seems little by little to have substituted work
among the poor for that of her work with
women in confinement. Whatever strength her
penitence left her she gave to them. At the home
of a patrician friend named Diabella she
founded a hospital which in 1286 became the
Hospital of Saint Mary of Mercy. Brother
Giunta assures us that Margaret consecrated
all her property, both personal and real, to this
foundation, keeping nothing back. But the
death of her lover must have left her without
resources. And had she not already stripped
herself of everything for the poor?

A brotherhood of men and women, doubtless associated with the Third Order, joined
her. They also helped the prisoners whom the
town would have let die of hunger if the faithful had not fed them. The regulations of the
brotherhood were drawn up on November 4th,
1286, in Saint Andrew's church. It was pre-
sided over by a prior aided by six rectors and

six advisers who remained in charge for six
months and who appointed their successors.
The associates of Margaret were called "the
poor little ones."

Margaret died in 1297 in a very humble
cell on Mount Sant-Egidio. It had been revealed to her in a dream at the foot of the
citadel. She knew that God wanted her there
and it was the object of bitter arguments with
those to whom she owed obedience.

We hope to be able to straighten out the
circumstances of a mystical order and the
events of that life that Brother Giunta has
given us almost haphazardly. The great temptation would be to group them according to the
laws set forth by the contemplatives. Thus, we
would see Margaret advancing by degrees from
the purgative life to contemplation, then to
spiritual marriage. And it is true that on God's
side a regular increase of graces was apparent
in His relations with the saint; thus, the first
words that Christ addressed to her marked the
end of the purgative stage; she was to enter,
with the ecstasy she had experienced on hear-

ing the Lord call her His daughter, into the
contemplative life. Finally, her last years, despite dreadful ordeals, reveal her to us as being
as lost in God as a living creature can be. It
seems that she attained the ineffable union directly, without passing through the "intellectual visions" which Saint Theresa has described.

But to examine closely the legend written
by Brother Giunta, it appears that a rigorous
classification of the episodes that he reports can
be only arbitrary. From the very first day
Margaret had given herself completely, and, to
the end, her destiny kept up an eddying of love
around the Crucified One, a self-hatred pushed
to the point of madness, an ever renewed
anxiety about not being pardoned. On the way
from the Celle to Cortona Margaret had already attained a degree of love that was un-
surpassable, but, until the year of her death, the
Master, in revenge, did not grant that a great
calm should reign in that soul which had been
overwhelmed with tenderness and terror. With
the result that the confusion, with which one

might be tempted to charge Brother Giunta, may render more faithfully what the life of this saint really was than would an order imposed upon it from without in accordance with the consecrated rules of mystic ascension.

Brother Giunta's indifference to chronology hardly shocks us in the tale of a life annihilated in God. Contemplation destroys the illusion of time. Margaret breathed in the eternal moment of that presence which enthralled her. And likewise it would serve no purpose, in our effort to know her better, to recall the manners and life of the age in which she lived. It would add nothing to our purpose to make us Guelf or Ghibelline, to take the part of Genoa against Venice, or Florence against Siena. As is a mystic of our own day, Margaret was a contemporary of Christ.

In whatever moment of history he may have lived, for the contemplative it is always the same confrontation, the same tête-à-tête, the same exigence of God, the same amorous effort of the fascinated creature. Margaret's dialogue with Christ, the heights and depths of her love, would have been the same a century earlier, six centuries later. Around this colloquy between the creature and the Creator there rages, roused by the same passions, the same human disorder, the same dismal slaughter from century to century.

CHAPTER VII

Ishmael or the Child Martyr

A TIME ALWAYS COMES WHEN WE LONG TO commit again the basest action we have committed, the one whose shame we feel most. The return to the vomit is a law of our nature, so shameful that thought turns aside from it. But, during his first steps in Grace, let a Christian beware of this temptation by which, sooner or later, he will be assailed!

The great mystics do not know of these humiliating renewals of desire. True sanctity never again desires to do the evil which it never ceases to expiate. Margaret, still a sinner on the way to Cortona, already felt, in regard to her errors, that absolute horror with which she would be possessed, without giving way, to her last breath.

34

And yet, a remnant of her execrable youth obtruded itself on Margaret; a heritage she could not renounce, and could not even keep herself from loving—the boy, the little fellow, who had perhaps the look, the gestures, the laugh of the murdered lover. Margaret, to the point of hallucination, found the father in the son. It was her living crime that pressed against her, that threw its arms about her neck; sometimes, she had to push him away with a violence that left the child flabbergasted and in tears. What could he understand of the unbelievable change in that charming and adored mother who had all at once become a poor woman, and who seemed to hate him?

And it is true that she did hate him while cherishing him; for this little being existed and breathed only insofar as she had mortally sinned against her God. But this God, was it not He Who had hurled scorn at the wisdom of men, at their reasonable morality?

What further had she to seek? But this son of her sin, he was so weak, so unprotected. So, being unable to make up her mind to separate from him, she took him along with her into her penitence. As did Agar to the little Ishmael, she fiercely carried him to the desert and condemned him to share her thirst.

He followed this beggar about in the streets, this beggar who begged only for poor people less poor than himself and who made him jealous. For nothing was too good for them; with her own hands she prepared rich foods and fish for them; but to the child she said, "My son, when you take possession of the cell where you will live hereafter, you will eat in silence the coarse foods that are intended for you. It is unfitting that I waste the time that is intended for praising God in preparing them."

She had distributed all her household utensils to the needy and kept no more than some old junk. When she had nothing more she went begging for linen for them, for clothes, wood, blankets, knives, pots, and glasses. She went so far as to cut off the sleeves of her dresses, gave them her veil, her chaplet, her holy-water basin, her very bedstead. But as for the child, he lacked everything. He never shared in the simple meals she prepared for the poor. Brother Giunta writes severely, "She was no more concerned about him than if she had not been his mother."

It would have been unbearable if she had been acting out of hardness of heart; but she fought against her heart with all her strength. One day it seemed to her that the Lord told her, "If you renounce yourself and your son, I shall call you my sister." So her little child was bound to her insofar as she could not renounce herself without renouncing him. Shall we yield to the temptation of saying, "These are hard words, and who can heed them?" But what the saints love in Christ's teaching is both what gives comfort to their nature and what outrages it and forces it to rebel.

We do not know what it is to believe. When Abraham agreed to sacrifice his son and had already tied the boy's hands, he reached an extremity of faith which horrifies us. And yet even at that moment, a few seconds before the angel held back his arms, he believed that his God was a God of love and comfort; likewise, Margaret did not doubt that, whatever the ordeal imposed upon the child of her sin, he was doubly beloved; first, because he was a man,

and there was not one whom Christ did not love
enough to die for; but also because he was the
son of a mother whom the Lord had chosen
from among many others, whom He had
snatched violently from guilty pleasures to become Himself her sole pleasure.

When she reflected on the words, "If any
man come to me, and hate not his father and
mother and wife and children and brethren and
sisters, yea and his own life also, he cannot be
my disciple," she turned neither her mind nor
heart away; she was not disturbed, knowing
that it was Love incarnate which taught her
those things.

No, this hatred desired by God does not resemble the hatred which gnaws at our sad lives.
God will take good care of those whom He asks
us to abandon, and it turns out that our sacrifice serves them better than does our selfish
attachment. We do not quite know what we owe
to some one who has given us up for Christ's
love. This aspect of the human drama escapes
the novelists and dramatists. A beloved woman
who resists or who, having yielded, makes
amends and renounces her passion, perhaps

saves her accomplice for all eternity; but he believes that he has been betrayed.

And the poor child, did he think himself betrayed? Young as he still was, Margaret had told him as much as he could understand of the story of his own life. There is no doubt that she introduced him to the mystery of the cross and that she told him as did Christ the son of Zebedee, "My chalice indeed you shall drink." It is not rare for a child to understand those things that he will no longer understand when he has become a man, for the kind of genius that strikes so many boys and which disappears with the awakening of the flesh also exists in regard to holiness. That simple expression, "holy childhood," conceals strange depths.

He must have let himself be persuaded by his God-possessed mother without resisting. Even if she had not been so visibly the prize of Grace he would have trusted her. . . . Remember: our mother was always right; she could not be mistaken; she did not have to be a saint to partake of divine infallibility.

CHAPTER VIII

The Temptation of Disgrace

SO, KEEPING BACK HIS TEARS, ISHMAEL FOL-
lowed his mother to the land of thirst and
hunger. He had to be, with full willingness of
heart, a child martyr.

But, whether it was God's will, we remain
free to doubt. We are not sure that Margaret
was not deceiving herself in this. Hagiography
exalts the saints as if they no longer shared in
the human condition. To tell the truth, to the
extent that they are lovers, that they are literally mad with love, the saints, like the rest of
us, remain subject to strange and terrible mistakes. If Margaret was mistaken in what concerned her son, it was not despite her love for
Christ, but by the very reason of that love.

Lacordaire has said that there are not two
kinds of love. When profane passion, the source

of so many crimes, turns away from creatures to attach itself to God, it retains its power to cause trouble. Jacques Rivière has observed in his journals of captivity, "No other religion has made love, with its flagrant disorders, its extravagant logic, all the disturbances it brings to the soul, intervene between the worshipper and God." Even when possessed with the love of God human nature remains weak and blind. A penitent, thirsting for humiliations, submits to the attraction of a sacrifice exceeding all others, one which, far from winning the world's praise, excites scorn and disgust.

For there can be no doubt that in all this Margaret yielded to the temptation of disgrace. She whose happiness it had been to have the praetor's soldiers slap her face and spit on it did not have the comfort of already being venerated as a saint. But in rejecting her son, here she was suddenly cutting a figure as a bad mother, a thing the world pardons least in a woman.

Margaret was visibly intoxicated with the horror that she aroused; this is apparent through the embarrassed commentary of

Brother Giunta. He echoes the slander then current in Cortona: "It was reported that the son whom she had abandoned and left in the deepest misery was seized with grief and had thrown himself into a well at Arezzo." It had been enough, to give some semblance of truth to this invention, that the child had not come to Cortona during the Christmas holidays, and that for some time he had been looked for in the schools of Arezzo without being found.

That year, the day when the church was celebrating the feast of Saint John the Evangelist, the child's teacher entered Margaret's oratory. After having taken communion, she was at prayer. He brought her news of the child and, at the same time, asked for payment for his work. Now, the Lord Who had forbidden Margaret to approach the Holy Table on the morning of the Nativity so that she might endure this feast in tears, had appointed the day of Saint John the Evangelist for her communion, but He had charged her to speak to no one on that day. So she made no answer to the teacher (whom Brother Giunta calls a teacher of elocution). "The latter, irritated, began to

mumble, and, in a voice bitter with anger, with
a look full of contempt, he accused her, in the
presence of the Minorites, of pride and ingrati-
tude. During this outburst, Margaret, undis-
turbed, was unwilling to say a word, though she
was begged by the brothers themselves to
answer. As for me, her unworthy confessor,
and Brother Benigno of blessed memory, we insisted, in order to force her to speak." But
Margaret did not wish to obey her worldly masters, for within she heard Christ say to her, "I
shall see whether you answer this man; I shall
see whether you prefer any creature to Me."
"No, my Lord," she replied, "I shall not dis-
obey You by speaking to anyone whatever." The
teacher might shout, the brothers might command; Margaret remained silent. Tired of
quarreling, the teacher finally left. Immediately
Jesus said, "Behold, My daughter, with what
strength I have endowed you! How sweet for
your soul it has been to maintain silence!"

CHAPTER IX

The Director Directed

BROTHER GIUNTA WAS WRONG TO URGE HER TO speak in this situation, since she considered herself bound, by a particular wish of Christ, to remain silent. But how had He allowed things to get to the point where Margaret no longer wanted to know anything about her son? The truth is that it is no longer a matter of direction when the one directed is a contemplative lost in God and the director a good simple monk without any personal experience in these mysteries.

A Saint John of the Cross, familiar with the loftiest spiritual states, would be able to speak as a master to penitents who are very advanced in the mystical life. But as for Brother Giunta Bevegnati we feel that he was both dazzled and dazed by this fiery soul.

Doubtless he would get to the point of restraining Margaret at the brink of the tortures which she dreamed of inflicting upon herself; he would even dare to forbid her certain too spectacular acts of penitence. But he almost always followed her where she wanted to go, anxious only not to let her out of sight, for she belonged to the Minorites, and they had to maintain their hold on her while she was alive in order to have her when she was dead. The Order watched jealously over its future relic, while Brother Giunta's big task was to collect the divine utterances that his penitent listened to, to filter them, to interpret them, to give them a certain tone. Did he not dwell too strongly on those which exalted the Minorites above all the orders and which sometimes flattered Margaret's director? But in the matter of the child, he allowed her to err. He does not seem to have discerned this obsession of hers, this happiness in being disgraced. What other reason could she have given for so scandalous an attitude? Even without interfering with extreme penitence, she would have been able to apply herself to the education of her son. In the

reign of Henry the Fourth, Madame Acarie, a
French bourgeoise, already overwhelmed with
ecstasy, and stigmatized, raised six children
strictly and rigorously. She waited until she had
straightened out her husband's affairs in order
to introduce the Carmelite reforms into
France.

The time that Margaret would have devoted to her son would not have been stolen
from God, and her taking care of him would not
have exempted her from practicing absolute
detachment in regard to him. She would have
loved him certainly, but as her fellow-creature
and not with the love of the flesh. Her tenderness toward him would have been mingled and
lost in the immense love she gave up to Christ.
It must have been to this effect that Saint John
of the Cross, at a later time, (addressing cloistered and not secular nuns) said, "In regard to
all persons, have the same love, have the same
indifference, whether relations or strangers.
Detach your heart as much from the one as
from the other; in a sense, even more particularly from relations, for fear lest flesh and
blood be stirred with the normal love which

must be forever mortified if one is to achieve spiritual perfection."

Perhaps Brother Giunta was already teaching that doctrine to his penitent. But for Margaret there was no question of father or mother, or of a son who was becoming a man. What woman could love only in God the child she has brought into the world? Perhaps Madame Acarie, perhaps a great French bourgeoise, but not this flaming Italian.

CHAPTER X

The Child of Sin with the Cowl

MARGARET FELT HERSELF AS INCAPABLE OF NOT sacrificing all to the beloved Christ, even her son, as of abandoning this son to the world which she had left behind with the pretext of thinking about him no further, except in her prayers. Whence that madness of taking him with her in that ascent forbidden to weak souls, without even troubling to find out whether he had the strength to follow her.

A remark of Christ which she heard on the feast day of Saint John the Evangelist is testimony of the fact that she never ceased to love him, to suffer for him: "Know that your troubles will increase and that your son *who shall be saved* will be one of the causes of your martydom." For us that is enough; we know that the mother was not so detached that the child, "son of so many tears," did not stay at the center of the martyrdom that she underwent. Margaret alone could have told what the cost to her was of this promise of salvation which the Lord had given her. While the world was scandalized and perhaps still is, she remained silent; but day after day she gave her blood to the child she was accused of abandoning, and she begot him in grief to lead him to eternal life.

Once accused, the saints are defeated in advance, because, the cross being a kind of mania, the motives of their acts escape logic, and they can give no reasons for them. Before Herod they can only keep the silence of the mocked Lord.

"Your son, who will be saved, will be one of the causes of your martyrdom." These words have another significance. We feel that the son of the sinner, he too, continued to the end to be submitted to an inhuman ordeal. For the Lord would not have taken the trouble to reassure Margaret concerning the salvation of the child if she had not had some reasons for having doubts about the matter, and it is this anguish

which added to her martyrdom. But Brother
Giunta informs us that the boy entered the
house of the Minorites. Margaret must have
felt great joy at that. She would have experienced only an increase of suffering if the little
one had fought against a rule which he had not
freely chosen or to which he had subjected himself to please his mother and because there was
no other way out.

Brother Giunta has preserved for us the
letter she wrote to the young novice when he became a monk: "My son, may God bless you in
the service to which you are devoting yourself,
and if, out of love for Him, you fight coura-
geously in the ranks of His soldiers, you will always have my affection. I shall be your mother
if you faithfully observe what I teach you.
First, I beg you, out of love for Christ our Lord
to plant deeply in your soul humbleness of
obedience and respect for the brothers, being
submissive to each one according to his rank
and having no preference for whoever it may
be. . . . Hide nothing from your confessor
that he should know. . . . A sick man can be
cured only by revealing his wounds. . . . Let

your speech be imbued with gentleness and
purity. Keep your senses from all sin. Read
often this letter which I send you. Keep it until
your death."

If the novice had had the strength to follow such advice, how could he have added to
the martyrdom of his mother? It is true that he
might have abandoned himself to debauchery
before entering the convent. . . . All this is
only conjecture. But a young monk whose salvation is in question—we know what that means.

Could Margaret, who had no fear of involv-
ing a child in her penitence, have been able to
imagine that when he reached the age of man-
hood he would remain free to change his path?
Moreover, there is nothing to indicate that he
kicked up his heels. No life was imaginable for
him but that of the cloister, no family but that
of the Minorites. Swept up in the wake of this
ascension, lifted up from the earth, he followed
from afar, agreed to everything. Was he not,
at one and the same time, the child of a guilty
love and the son of one of the blessed, born of
the two loves which had possessed Margaret,
torn between the inclinations of a flaming

nature and the demands of the terrible Grace
of which his mother was the prey and which,
through her, reached him and snatched him
from the world?

The only anecdote that Brother Giunta has
related about him illuminates the strife between
the frail good-will of the novice and an unconsciously rebellious flesh and spirit: "One
night, Margaret's son, overcome with sleep,
did not awake to say matins with the brothers.
The Father Superior went to wake him with a
little rod, with which he lightly tapped him as
a father might. But the young man, awakened
by force, began to scream and snatched the rod
from the father's hand for fear of being struck
further. At once seized with regret for this act,
he tore at his face with the pointed hood of his
tunic." Margaret, informed by an inner vision,
sent for him and gently reproached him.

No one in the world exudes more quiet joy
than a good monk. Although the peace which
he tastes is the peace of Christ, an austere peace
to which the man remains attached as does the
crucified One to the cross, the religious life,
penetrated by the eternal, benefits no less from

this miracle of being in the fleetingness of the moment—a river at its estuary, already commingled with the shoreless sea.

But there are other monks. . . . At the outset of certain sacerdotal careers, errors of sidetracking occur (in the seminary more often than in the novitiate). What good is it to conceal those tragic cases where it is quite a delicate matter to balance lack of judgment among the directors and faithlessness to Grace among the directed? In this uninterrupted labor of Grace on nature, everything pertaining to man, pervaded by and seized by infinite love, remains a tributary of the nothingness which is his own. Whence those miscarriages, those human wastes which encumber the paths of Heaven. In the ditches, what corpses half gnawed away by the wild beasts! What bones there are, buried in the sand!

If there is nothing in what we have reported which proves conclusively that the son of Margaret was a bad monk, everything leads us to fear that he was a tormented monk. Born in sin, caught up in the eddies of an immense love, he shared in the penitence which was atoning

for sin. Had he lived like a criminal, but happy
by worldly standards, his fate would not have
moved us. Margaret knew what her accusers
were unaware of, that in casting him into the
sea, she was casting him at God. The child's
destiny could not help being fulfilled within
Christ's love for Margaret and Margaret's for
Christ. In that deadly struggle, nobody was responsible for his being a piece on the chess-
board; he was caught, with no conceivable escape, between the two adversaries.

And if that shocks our morality, let us have
the courage to confess that the saints scoff at
our morality. Tête-à-tête with her God, Margaret suffered and burned beyond all wisdom, all
human rules, as alone with Him as was Abraham beneath the oaks of Mamre, mindful of
the divine exigence alone in what concerned
the child of her guilty love.

Face to face with the Eternal, beyond all
reasonable morality. . . . Even the simple believer has some notion of the tragedy of this
solitude. It is not necessary to hear inner words
nor to know ecstasy in order to understand the
meaning of that Grace which, during the inter-

val of duration, binds us, ephemeral creatures
that we are, to the uncreated being. There is no
railing around the moment of the state of
Grace; a single look, a single thought, a single
desire; there need be no more than that, and
we fall from Heaven like a thunderbolt; it is
merely enough to want to for us to be hurled
down.

Who would dare deny that, without any
particular temptation, the believer sometimes
dreams of closing his eyes and allowing himself
to slip into the abyss, for no other reason than
to break up this exhausting tête-à-tête, for no
other reason than to escape from a love which,
humble as it may make itself, is, nevertheless,
incommensurate with our cowardice?

"Watch and pray." The wretched soul
dreams of an irremediable state of despair in
which it can at last sleep, in which there will be
no one to pray. . . . Oh love! How dare one
write these things? It is not that Love itself is
no longer loved. For the fearful soul it is a matter of breaking up the tête-à-tête and rejoining
God by another route, one which, through forbidden lands, ends in mercy. As if this journey

could be carried through without a frightful risk! We know them, those routes strewn with the corpses of suicides.

In strictly keeping her son in cowl and ashes, Margaret knew what she was doing.

CHAPTER XI

The Gloomy Daughter
of Joyous Francis

THIS, HOWEVER, ASTONISHES US: THE MARGA-
ret who presented so formidable a face to her
child belonged to the Third Order of Saint
Francis and it was the Minorites who guided
her. She lived in the very region which the poor
little seraphic one had frequented fifty years
earlier. She was able to hear his companions
preach.

Assisi is not far from Cortona. Saint Francis, accompanied by Brother Sylvester had
come there in 1221; he had converted the famous Brother Elia who was to direct the Order
and turn it from its primitive observances; but
the saint had made a better conquest at Cortona
in the person of Guido Vagnotelli, a rich young

man who had received Francis and his companions as angels of God.

Aided by Guido and Brother Sylvester, Francis founded the Celle on the bank of a stream which flows from Sant-Egidio. He returned there a short time before dying. He left it with Brother Elia who took care of him; his hands, his legs, his stomach were swollen; his stomach rejected all food. It was necessary, therefore, to take him back to Assisi.

When in 1245, Brother Elia founded the monastery of Cortona where Margaret was later to find her protectors and guides, the blessed Guido Vagnotelli lived with a few brothers in the poor convent of the Celle, and it was there that Margaret, wounded by love, instinctively went to humble herself.

Even at the time of her sins, the young woman had to steep herself in Franciscan holiness. Before there was any pardon, Grace delivered her over to the Minorites. But it was not for the purpose of turning her away from the harshest mortification. It almost goes without saying that the excess of her penitence did not keep her from becoming a true daughter of

Saint Francis. On the contrary, we recognize by this sign that she is of his family.

Francis' joy, his love of animals and plants, the gift he had of making inanimate nature alive, the angelic power of chasing off the pagan deities, of baptizing great Pan, of chaining the rain, the fire, the wind, his brother the sun and his sisters the stars, to the triumph of the Son of man, the exultation of the inspired poet who reconciles within himself the creatures and the Creator, make us unmindful of his pitiless asceticism. We no longer discern, through the fragrant tales of the *Fioretti* the half blind, enfeebled man who waged so harsh a struggle against his body that at the end he himself took pity on "his brother the ass," as he called it; and one of his last wishes before dying was to grant a childish pleasure to this poor brother; he wanted to taste an almond and sugar pastry, *mostaccioli,* that his friend Jacoba de Settesoli had brought him from Rome; but he could hardly touch it.

The Franciscan joy is such that the world no longer sees the stigmata of the poverello and forgets that this other Christ is dead, he too

crucified. As long as he lived, that joy concealed from his brothers and the people the real
face of the poverty to which he was so strictly
married. When he was no longer there and his
disciples saw her face to face, many became
frightened before this horribly stripped and
fleshless spouse. There was then a merciless
struggle between the ascetics, the true heirs of
the little Poor One, and those who wanted their
reasonable salvation. Implacable poverty became a sign of contradiction, not only in the
Order, but in the entire church.

Margaret was born, lived, and suffered in
the midst of this furious war of which, before
her birth, Cortona was the center (since
Brother Elia of Cortona, the successor of Saint
Francis, became head of the enemies of Holy
Poverty).

And certainly we believe we can see which
side Margaret inclined toward at the very
start, she who instinctively ran to the extreme
of privation, and who followed Francis into the
"furnace" where, as he himself said, love had
placed him. But at the same time she remained
faithful to the church and thereby separated

herself from the irreconcilables, the foes of the simoniacal popes and ostentatious cardinals, those for whom the coming of Francis had been like a new incarnation. The "fraticelles" held obedience to Rome cheap; they were waiting for the conflagration of the world by the Spirit, as Joachim of Flore had prophesied. The example of boldness had come to them from higher up. Who doubts that Saint Anthony of Padua, so fresh and ruddy, to whom good women today mutter prayers to find their purses, the formidable enemy of the straddling Elia of Cortona, thundered against the dissoluteness of the Roman court with a violence that Savonarola was later to imitate and that no heretic has ever surpassed.

The penitence of Margaret differs from that of the seraphic Father on this point; joy does not hide horror. Although Francis never ceased to weep for the mistakes of his youth and though he too went through days of anguish and agony, the memory of his errors could not avail against his happiness. It was a far cry from the folly of the prince of the youth of Assisi to that nine-year union when Marga-

ret was a public sinner. The somewhat intoxicated adolescent that Francis had been did not
ceaselessly pursue him, did not haunt all his
nights. As for Margaret, she always kept her
past shame with her. Not that she doubted
God's love, but rather, it was her love for herself which was pitiless and which refused itself
the pardon it had received. For the wrongs inflicted upon her beloved for nine years she
could not console herself.

Yet there is nothing of a gloomy and sterile
fury in her penitence. She entered an order,
she had a reason to do so, an aim, fruits whose
benefits infinitely surpass the person of the
creature who inflicts the penitence on himself.
At the beginning, the spirit of penitence drove
her on; but if she had no other purpose than
expiating her error, her hand would doubtless
have tired of striking. The truth is that she
sought with patient zeal to relieve the sufferings of her crucified Lord. Her last ambition
was not to live a longer life than did Christ.

At this point we must recall the saying of
Lacordaire, but only for the purpose of con-
tradicting it: "There are not two loves." For

nothing less resembles the love which Christ
inspires in his lovers than does human passion.
Like her father Francis, like all the friends of
Christ, Margaret aspired to be in conformity
with her God; she violated nature only to attain this conformity. On the contrary, the
drama of the human passion, the shocks, the
disputes, the misunderstandings, the ruptures,
the whole wretchedness, comes from the fact
that each of the lovers remains himself, resists
the others, makes demands, is exacting, and
that the blending, the loss of one's identity in
the other, is achieved only for a moment, by a
short embrace.

CHAPTER XII

A Fearful Grace

AT THE BEGINNING OF HER PENITENCE, THE absolution which gives a feeling of deliverance to ordinary Christians increased Margaret's grief. How could she have done what she had done? Her sobs would awaken those who slept near her cell. "The Eternal is a jealous God," she would repeat, a formidable God Who scrutinizes closely the souls he has created. Repentance incited her to consider only the judge in the incarnate love which had not yet reassured her with its words. She had to pass through this anguish.

Even during the early period of her colloquies with Christ, she was more than once rudely brought back by Him to the horror of her past life. One day when, in tears, she humbly asked Him to give her the name of daughter, just as He called her "poor little one," suddenly the voice broke forth terribly, "I shall not yet call you My daughter because you are the daughter of sin." However, He promised her that as soon as she would be purified by a general confession He would place her in the ranks of His beloved daughters.

Then she received a favor of Grace which seems terrible when one tries in imagination to apply it to himself; the Lord made her see distinctly all the mistakes of her life, one by one, down to the smallest sin of thought. For the average worshipper there is no doubt that the faculty of forgetfulness which is granted him is the will of God. How could we continue to live with those acts and desires of ours, from the time we began to do evil, always swarming about us? "If you knew your sins," Jesus said to Pascal, "you would lose heart." So He did not lay them bare before him. However, He had no fear of overwhelming a poor penitent woman with what He spared the weakness of the greatest genius, because He measured what she was capable of enduring.

Mary of the Incarnation, a French saint,

whose life had always been innocent, went through the same ordeal and almost died of it. "In one moment," she cried, "the eyes of my spirit were opened, and all the errors, sins, and imperfections of which I had been guilty since coming into the world were spread out before me in full detail, with a distinctness and clearness more certain than any certainty of human skill could inspire. At the same moment I saw myself completely plunged in blood and my mind was convinced that it was the blood of the Son of God, for the spilling of which I was guilty because of all the sins which had been spread out before me, and that this precious blood had been shed for my salvation. Had not the goodness of God sustained me, I should have died of fright."

In the light of this revelation, which left in doubt nothing of what she had committed, or merely dreamed of committing, Margaret needed not less than a week to complete her general confession. The following day, with the rope around her neck, and with no veil on her head, she tremblingly approached the holy table. Hardly had she received the host when suddenly a voice burst forth at her, "My daughter!" Margaret, who, without losing courage, had endured seeing everything she was ashamed of rise up from oblivion, swooned on hearing the name "daughter" for the first time. She fell to the floor in ecstasy. Brother Bevegnati was there as well as Brother Rinaldo and Brother Ubaldo. Every now and then she came to her senses. "I am His daughter," she kept repeating. "He said so!" The witnesses heard her stammer, "Oh, infinite gentleness of my God! Oh, word so long desired! so urgently besought! Ocean of joy! My daughter! It is my God Who said so! My daughter! It is my Jesus Who calls me thus!"

It was her first ecstasy. On the cries of love which escaped her, the worshippers rushed up and, doubtless, the people in the street as well. It would serve no purpose to recall that this took place in thirteenth-century Italy, for holiness still creates the same eddyings of the crowd to-day. Theresa Neumann, a Bavarian woman who bore the stigmata, lived in the same atmosphere of veneration and pious curiosity as Margaret of Cortona. Our Saint suffered at making such a spectacle of herself. Perhaps she already knew that ecstasies are imperfections which give proof of our weak human nature. She ardently desired the secret for her love, solitude with God. Moreover, the excessiveness of her penance soon reduced her to being unable any longer to leave her residence without a great deal of suffering. She therefore asked Christ for permission not to leave her cell; but He severely reproved her, "Why do you ceaselessly ask to taste of My delights and why do you refuse the tribulations? Go and think no more of hiding yourself until I allow you to take leave of the world."

At dawn she dragged herself to the Brothers' church and there at once dropped to the floor with joy. She was still there at twilight, flooded with peace.

CHAPTER XIII

The Dishevelled Magdalene

AT THE SAME TIME AS HE COMPELLED HER
not to conceal herself, the Lord forbade her to
speak to lay people, except in case of necessity.
There is nothing so dangerous as a sanctified
soul's consciousness of its progress. If it was
necessary for Margaret to remain exposed to
view in order to edify those who observed her,
it was still more important for her not to
yield to vainglory. But we know that she was
tempted in this respect; she had to struggle
against the thought that Christ had adorned
and enriched her with all the virtues, that He
had made her famous to the point of being
visited by multitudes!

In order to overcome this temptation she
had recourse to a strange means, one which is
proof enough that, despite what I said earlier,

it would be absurd not to take into account the
country or the race of our saint. Doubtless, a
saint is, first of all, a contemporary of Christ;
beneath all skies and in all ages she withers
away alone in the world facing her Creator.
And yet, for all that, what Margaret did at
Cortona to conquer the angel of vainglory is
conceivable only in Italy and in Italy of the
thirteenth century. "She waited for the silence
of night," says Brother Bevegnati, "and when
everybody was sleeping peacefully, she got up
on the roof of the building where her cell was
and there, amidst cries and sobs, cried out,
'Inhabitants of Cortona, awake, and, without
wasting time, chase me from your region with
stones, because I am the sinner who is guilty
of excesses of all kinds.' Amidst tears, she told
the residents of the neighborhood who had been
awakened by her cries about the errors of her
past life, to such an extent that, moved and
edified, they burst into tears and gave up
thanks to God."

We do not know what is more astonishing,
this impetuous saint, like the disheveled Magdalene who cries aloud, at Venice, in the last

painting of the aged Titian (the one which death did not permit him to finish) or the good folk who, torn from their sleep, instead of cursing and wishing her to the devil, showed only compassion for her, without dreaming of being scandalized or laughing at a humility capable of such an outburst. They did not protest to her that the only one of her excesses that they could rightly judge unpardonable was precisely the one which kept them from sleeping. Could such a lover, sobbing and twisting, her arms beneath the stars, inviting the whole town to the spectacle of her repentance, have been born elsewhere than in the country which saw the birth of the opera? One may muse, despite himself and not without a little irreverence, that there is a bit of *bel canto* of saintliness in this and that the chorus of the residents of the neighborhood replies to the nocturnal solo of the prima donna . . . But the wonder is that we are not at the theatre, that this saint and the people of Cortona display in utter simplicity the feelings by which they are moved.

Nevertheless, some readers will have their own private thoughts about this sort of thing;

for example, that the angel of vainglory could have found just what he was looking for in this demonstration which was ostensibly directed against him.

What saint among us would have been capable of conceiving this stage setting? (I think back to Mary of Valence of whom Abbé Brémond tells us "that she did not like to play the saint.") We would resist the thought, "What preoccupation with self! What importance conferred upon her own person!" . . . if Margaret's directors had similarly felt the danger.

On the subject of Saint Francis' dispute with his father, the Bishop of Assisi remonstrated with him, Chesterton tells us, "with that excellent good sense that the Catholic church keeps in permanent reserve against the fiery attitudes of her saints." Brother Bevegnati's excellent Catholic good sense was put to a hard trial by his penitent whose confession under the stars did not at all quench her thirst for public humiliations.

Margaret begged her confessor for permission to return to Montepulciano; she wanted to reappear where she had once lived in luxurious

garments, her hair adorned with gold chains,
going out only on horseback or in a carriage,
her face made up, proud of her lover's wealth;
but now she wanted to appear there with
shaven head, dressed in rags, and begging from
door to door; and fearing that she might not
be recognized, she wanted a woman to lead her
by a rope as if she were blind and to cry aloud,
"My friends, this woman is Margaret whose
vainglory, whose morals, have injured so many
among you."

But the good brother, who without any
doubt would have forbidden the confession on
the roof had he been consulted, stoutly opposed
this ostentatious journey. He let Margaret
know that she would do better to put a check
on undertakings of such indiscreet fervor and
he forbade her to do anything more about
this project. However, Margaret insisted and
finally received permission to return, not to
Montepulciano, but to Laviano where she had
been born. "There, at the time of mass, in the
presence of the whole assembled population,
with a rope around her neck, prostrated at
the feet of a woman named Manentessa, she

begged for pardon, flooded in a torrent of tears."

None of these excesses disturbed Brother Bevegnati, but at length, when he deemed them worthy of condemnation, he did condemn them. One day when she conceived a penance which exceeded in horror anything that her mad love had yet inspired, he went so far as to threaten her that he would no longer hear her confession.

CHAPTER XIV

The Wild Act of Love

EVER SINCE THE DOOR-KEEPER OF THE CELLE
had said to her, "You are too pretty," Margaret had fought fiercely against her beauty.
But certain faces are indestructible; the mortifications affected the flesh only and could do
nothing to that harmony which is in the very
bone structure of a well-built face.

Margaret had turned the zeal which women
apply to beautifying themselves against that
invincible charm which still astonished her (did
she therefore have a mirror?) . The rage which
their ugliness keeps alive in the ugly she felt
because of her tenacious beauty, but multiplied
ten-fold by the very force of the love which
inspired her with it. Imagine Brother Bevegnati's terror when his penitent showed him a
razor and begged him for permission to slash
her face, nose, and lips. In vain did she promise

not to wound herself mortally; he did not allow her to do it and threatened to dismiss her from his confessional and that of the other brothers as well. Margaret immediately threw away the razor.

The only thing that should count for us is what inspired this wild act—a wonderful love. "Fiery God, You in Whom all excess is permitted . . ." This line of a profane poet is far-reaching. What is common to all the saints is a love which seeks conformity with the cross of the beloved Lord; however, each of them has his difficulties, his own particular obstacles. The holocaust is the same, but not the victim. Some other contemplative, lacking in physical seductiveness and never having loved or been loved carnally, knows nothing of this appetite for destruction and those audacities of holy vengeance.

But there is more; asceticism precedes all holiness and even all reform. The ploughshare of penitence of her who mortifies the flesh directly must be dug in much more deeply as the instincts have been better satisfied, as pleasures have been more delightful.

Even outside of penitence, simple prudence requires the sanctified soul to enfeeble the body which for years was used to being the first to be served. Even when it has attained contemplation, and when there not only no longer remains any inclination for past crimes, but even when it has such a horror of them that it would rather die a thousand deaths than ever backslide, the body to which it is bound retains its instincts, habits, reflexes, a memory. It exists as a power of recollection, immanent in the flesh; the blood is full of remembrances.

So, some souls which, being too sure of their inclination toward the things of God, have yielded themselves up in full quietness and without bewaring any longer of their body, have known its terrible awakening.

From a spiritual point of view, nothing was less mad than the seeming folly of Margaret's insistence on destroying her too lovely face, and nothing was more mad than to aspire to reach God without having first subdued and subjugated her flesh and without having guarded against the return of indestructible lust.

Margaret remembered all that her body had

endured because of her coquetry. How many women go without food "to keep their figure" as they put it; and one sees them standing erect after meals during which they haven't touched a thing; or going in for painful exercises— even going through bloody operations. The world which is scandalized at the sufferings whose principle is love of God approves asceticism in the service of the devil; and it likewise excuses the deadly ravages of alcohol and drugs.

Margaret asked Brother Bevegnati, "How can this body of clay complain about being treated this way in God's service, since it would not complain if I used it in like manner to satisfy my vanity or to serve the world or the devil. As well trust a traitor, a murderer, or one's worst enemy as trust the body."

One day, when the good brother, in opposing excessive mortifications, begged her to take some food, she finally replied, "As there should never be a truce between my soul and my body, I have decided not to spare the latter; let me tear it to pieces, mortify it, up to the very last moment of my life, when I shall at last see it

separated from the soul. Do not think that it
is as weak and mortified as it seems. It puts on
a sham apathy in order to force me once more
to taste the delights and pleasure to which I
had accustomed it in the past."

Perhaps Margaret was here alluding to the
revenge that the flesh takes under cover of
night. The mystic lost in God, who lives iso-
lated from the world, protected at all his fron-
tiers, that of his eyes, his mouth, his thought—
what can he do against his dreams? As long
as his vigils at the feet of the Lord continue,
he can not defend himself against sleep, which,
for a few hours, disarms him. Then nothing
prevents the enemy, the sower of chaff, from
penetrating the sluggish soul. Everything is
asleep in the poor, faithful creature; everything is asleep but the body which pretends to
sleep. All is suspended, except the power of
producing images of what the soul hates and
the senses adore.

It is the hour of the angelic world—but,
thank God, not only the one which corrupts the
darkness. The soul in a state of grace sleeps
surrounded by angels. What God permits it to

undergo at times (so that it may remember the clay whereof it is kneaded and by which it is on all sides hemmed in), makes it more attentive to the mysterious protection of its nights. Besides, the angel which guards it often wakes it at the brink of involuntary crime.

And doubtless nothing counts which is performed outside of the will. But the enemy eagerly looks forward to the trouble he inflicts on us. Everything comes from us in spite of us. The most intimate part of us begets our dreams; they are the children of our flesh; the most hideous terrify us by a very secret resemblance.

This unknown bond rises to the surface of the sleeping soul. A beast which the faithful one believes dead goes forth from its lair under cover of night and walks about freely within the enchained creature. So everything which the soul thought to have forever smothered and destroyed is still there. The intercession of the Virgin and the Saints, how necessary they seem here! We can not protect ourselves all alone in those hours when all our powers are suspended, save the most base, those hidden deep

in our bowels . . . As if God wished that, all
the same, without crime, we might touch someone's shoulders, as if His mercy delivered the
faithful one to a contamination which, without
contaminating him, humbles and prostrates
him.

These things, which one avoids speaking
about, keep alive the vigilant hatred of the
saints who never think they have opposed suf-
ficiently the defeated but unsubdued flesh. Even
among the perfect ones there is a beast whose
door is left ajar every night by sleep.

Margaret was so distrustful of her body
that, being barely able to talk, to such an extent
had she mortified it, she feared that this state
was a pretense of the flesh which was feigning
an illness for the sake of getting some consolation. And one day, bursting into tears, she cried
out before her director, "Oh, my body, why
don't you help me serve your Creator and Redeemer? Why don't you have the same zeal to
obey Him as you once had to defy Him? Stop
your lamentations, stop feigning death. Bear
now the burden I put upon you as you once
bore your iniquities."

CHAPTER XV

Poor Soul, Never Assured

IF MARGARET NEVER SUSPECTED THAT SHE might be substituting her own voice for that of the Spouse, she feared that the enemy, disguised as an angel of light, might play a trick in revenge. It could not be, she thought, that God was speaking to the sinner of Montepulciano. The doorkeeper of the Celle had said, "You are too pretty," and he had shut the door. Would she ever forget that curse? Always having her crimes in mind, she refused to believe in the favors which overwhelmed her. It was necessary for Christ to reassure her constantly: "He Who speaks to you is He Whom you have crucified," and again, "Love yourself because I love you." And at times the Redeemer's love for the sinner broke out in words which almost frightened the tormented creature: "You are My daughter because you have obeyed Me. You are My spouse because I am your only love. You are My mother because you fulfill, to the extent of your powers, the will of My father . . . There is no other on earth whom I love more than you." She protested, stammered, "Do not trust me who have been and still am nothing but darkness." Thinking of all the time that her love had wasted, she groaned, "I have come to You too late; too late did I begin to love You." Then He reassured her, "Too late? But how promptly! Too late because you delayed . . . But what a fervor was yours!"

Sometimes Margaret did not at first understand the meaning of certain words. One morning after communion she heard the Lord sigh, "Enjoy yourself, My soul!" Was He talking to Himself or was He addressing her? But He did not leave her long in doubt, for He continued, "Enjoy yourself, daughter of Jerusalem, for I have chosen your soul to set up My dwelling. Praise Me, I shall praise you. Love Me, I shall love you. Serve Me, I serve you and shall serve you."

Then was her joy overflowing. A servant
helped her in her weakness. She covered Margaret's head with a veil made of pieces of cloth
sewn together. She often divided these with the
poor. It even happened that she stripped herself to the point of remaining naked in her cell,
rolled up in a cane matting. Raw herbs, nuts,
almonds, that was all she ate. She wept during
meals, and remained with her mind a blank,
forgetting to eat. As she could no longer remain standing after having taken communion,
the Lord, taken with pity, sometimes said to
her, "You may lean your head on the hassock."

Someone whispers to me, "Aren't you tired
of this folly?" Sometimes one feels himself
weary at so constant an offense against nature.
The Lord's presence in a simple household,
children around the table, evening, the father
bends his heavy brow over the steaming soup,
and the wife, who no longer feels tired, constantly gets up to serve them all. Detachment
from self, from one's own destiny, powerless-
ness to speculate about images, about dreams,
in the narrow cloister of a humble, physical
duty. Holiness of those poor women who don't

know what holiness is—loyal to the little ones
they have begotten and to the homely husband,
brutalized by his work, he too crucified but on
that cross where there is no glory, the work-
shop, the office.

You show us a crazy life which is like nothing that we have gone through. A stigmatized
hand has less meaning for us than a hand that's
chapped from laundering.

The truth is that there are only individual
vocations. God has willed that the love which
in a few chosen creatures manifests itself in a
pure state is mixed, for other destinies, with
the daily round of life. The vocation of a small
number of souls is to be consumed. A small
number of chosen victims agree to drain to the
dregs the chalice of which a few drops are
enough for the simple worshipper to become
worthy of the name "Child of God."

These sacrificed saints do not resign themselves to the superabundance of evil; they do
not accept Hell, though they believe in it. They
are torn with cries at what sin has made of
creation. They appeal to love, to their God Who
is Love. With sublime liberality they throw the

weight of their suffering on the scale to balance the world's crimes.

The ordinary Christian relishes his peace in accordance with the communion, dines with a bigger appetite, does his daily good deed quite properly, writes an edifying letter to a friend, minds his affairs, and watches the next fellow ruin himself with a pity which is not free from a certain obscure satisfaction. Allow some madly loving people to be unresigned to the loss of so many souls, to surrender themselves, to cast themselves into the fire so that the number of the elect may not be small! As much as I love Pascal, I hate in him that gloomy pleasure of being elected, when he feels sure that almost nobody else is; I hate the spiritual greed which makes him seek and relish the drop of blood that has been spilled for him alone, for him, not for the others. Did he, a Jansenist, ever cry out to his pitiless God, "I choose to be eternally lost in the innumerable crowd of those You have rejected"? The saints upset the cruel logic of Port Royal; they break up the system; they introduce their charming disorder into the calculations of predestination. Margaret, poor tortured woman, sometimes your mad actions repel us; but it is this madness which triumphs over the dungeon gates where, in the expectation of never-ending despair, we have had to expiate here below the crime of being ourselves.

CHAPTER XVI

Each Sheep Is the Preferred One But Does Not Know It

MARGARET'S CONTINUED TREMBLING, DESPITE the favors which were showered on her, were wished on her by the very One Who reproached her for it. He wanted to glorify her but without her glorifying herself. Humble as the penitent was, her humility had to resist overwhelming assurances: "You are My daughter, My friend whom I love above all women now living on earth."

Above all women! The French translator of Brother Bevegnati, strongly impressed by this statement, points out that Margaret was a contemporary of Saint Gertrude, Saint Angela of Foligno, Saint Julianna of Falconieri . . . To tell the truth, looking through the revela-

tions of Saint Gertrude, I fell almost at once
on these words of Christ concerning Gertrude:
"No man alive is closer to Me than this beloved
spouse. There is no creature on earth to whom
I turn with so much delight" (I, 3). The pious
translator has therefore been wrong in taking
literally the approximations which the com-
mentators give of God's ineffable words to His
chosen creatures. The increate love is given in
all its fulness to each one of them whom He has
spirited away from this world to the threshold
of the beatific vision; each ewe is the preferred
one.

But insofar as it is permitted to interpret
a wish of God, He wanted to glorify Margaret
without her thereby becoming proud. "He Who
is" overwhelms and fulfills "her who is not"
(according to what was said to Saint Catherine of Siena). The fulfilled creature must, at
no moment of her prodigious good fortune, lose
the certitude that she is nothing.

The strange thing is that this is how it is.
An ordinary Christian has difficulty in under-
standing that a holy soul, wrapped up in God,
forgets itself to the point of being disinterested

in what is taking place within itself and manages not to be dazzled by it.

One of the difficulties of the holy life is that the soul watches itself praying. Hardly has it been touched with fervor than it observes the fire which burns it; it listens to itself talking to God. Veracious as it may wish to be in the eyes of Him who probes their hearts, it hears the inner words which it utters, it is conscious of its attitude, it follows the progress of its tears, it anticipates the effect produced. How escape this playing with mirrors? The creature is present at his colloquy with the Creator and cannot help seeing its indefinitely multiplied effects.

It is proof that the poor soul has not even begun yet to lose self-consciousness. A Margaret of Cortona no longer sees herself; she appears mad only because she has lost sight of herself for some time, because she has lost almost all control over her behavior. The apparent madness of the saints is due to their being literally outside of themselves, but inside of another; they breathe, they move, within the infinite Being.

CHAPTER XVII

The Sinner Who Looks No Higher than the Cross

MORE THAN ANY OTHER CONTEMPLATIVE, MAR-
garet feared the danger of yielding to self-
complacence. The penitent used that past which
horrified her, that youth which, in her eyes,
was criminal, to shelter herself against pride,
self-love, the satisfaction of being loved by
God. A Gertrude who had never known any
other sheepfold or pasture than the convent,
whose confessions since childhood had doubtless been concerned with trifles, how unprotected against vanity she seems in comparison
with a Magdalene, a Margaret, or an Angela!
Old passions, a thousand times expiated, leave
scars which seem horrible in the light of pure
love. The further Christ advances in a soul, the

more closely does it see its blemishes and the better it understands the cost they have been to Him who has assumed them. Moreover, a contemplative penitent hardly contemplates Christ except in the agonies of her anguish; she never loses the awareness of the active part she personally played every moment of her criminal life. She lets others give their attention to the glorious Christ or, like Elisabeth of the Trinity, the little Carmelite of Dijon who died in 1906, live with the three Persons in a mysterious familiarity.

For it would be a mistake to think that all saints live like Margaret with their eyes fixed solely on the Cross. When the Spanish Anne of Jesus, the friend of Saint Theresa, came to France in 1604 to establish the Carmelite convent, the prayer of the first French Carmelites astonished her. "I am seeing to it that they heed and imitate Our Lord Jesus Christ," she wrote, "for He is very little remembered here. Everything takes place here with a simple view of God; I don't know how that can happen." And she was already denouncing the influence of the writings of Saint Denis. It is true that

Bérulle, who was the spiritual master of the
first French Carmelites, was particularly inter-
ested in the Father, as was the Jesuit Lallemant
in the Holy Ghost.

A daughter of Saint Theresa could be led
astray there. However, the exclusive attachment to the gloomy mysteries was not inflicted
upon all the Spanish mystics. Saint John of the
Cross once asked a nun what her prayer was,
and she answered that it was the contemplation
of the beauty and grandeur of God. The saint
was so happy about this answer that she inspired him to write the following strophe of the
Cantico: "Let us rejoice, beloved—and let us
go to see ourselves in your beauty—on the
mountain and on the hill—there where the pure
water gushes forth—let us proceed farther
into the thicket."

There are many dwellings on the highest
terrace of our Father's house. But the former
concubine of the Lord of Montepulciano, a
stranger to so sublime a prayer, breathed and
moved only beneath the olive-trees of agony,
in the dust of the praetorium; she kissed the
body of her God which was tied to a column,

bleeding with Him under the whiplashes; she mingled in the crowd while He dragged the gibbet whose weight was crushing Him. And it was Christ Himself Who showed her the place in His open heart, in His outraged flesh, crowned with thorns, hung from three nails.

Doubtless the humbled woman from Cortona, the repentant daughter-mother, knew those moments when one goes beyond visions and words; she too passed beyond everything on her way to meet God. But she always had to retrace her steps to kneel in the humble place which had been assigned to her, at the height of the pierced feet of Jesus Christ.

It was not at the approach of Holy Week, but during the octave of Epiphany that she heard this cry: "Return to My cross. Continue to weep at My feet; you ought neither to restrain nor hide your grief." One Easter day she was not invited to celebrate with the rest of the world the resuscitation of her God; but on the contrary the Lord Himself brought her back to meditation on the mournful mysteries. The Jesus of Margaret left His tomb only to

begin again the same excruciating ascent, and
He drew His penitent along after Him.

He did not reveal to her the unknown circumstances of His passion as He later did to
Catherine Emmerich. But He invited her to discover the particular place which each one of
us has occupied among the executioners. At the
words of the *Mystery of Jesus,* "I have shed
that drop of blood for you," Christ, through
the mouth of Margaret, allows each one of us
to answer, "And I gave you that lash, that slap;
that spit was mine."

And doubtless one rather feels a certain
method, certain ideas, in the back of the good
Brother Bevegnati's mind in the page I shall
quote; but how sublime it must have been, taken
at the source in its first bubblings.

"I shall tell you what those are who have
crucified Me. First, the Judases: those who
speak, eat, drink, sleep with men, in order to
assassinate them afterward. Those who strip
Me, who take My gown by lot. The highway
murderers. The Pharisee who condemns men on
false evidence and false charges, and has them

condemned is the same who brought Me before Pilate.

Who tears out My hair? The goldsmiths, the merchants, the artists, and all the money-lovers. Who whips Me and ties Me to the post? The bands in the camps and the forests, when they bind, whip and mutilate other men and demand ransom. To lay hands on priests and members of holy orders is to slap Me. To drive tenants from their houses, to reduce them to begging, thievery, fornication, is to stretch Me on a cross so short and narrow that I can not rest My head there.

Casuists crucify Me, and also iniquitous advisers, those who make unjust laws and against their conscience say, 'Act in this way.' Who hides his face like a thief? Fornicators and adulterers. Blasphemers spit in My face, and so do those who paint their faces. Who gives Me gall and vinegar to drink and tortures Me just short of death? He who yields to unnamable vice and to sins against nature.

Those who see My body at the altar and refuse to believe that I am there insult Me on the cross. Evil prelates are as bad as Herod and, like Herod, make game of Me. My mercy shields them now, but warn them that My justice will not spare them.

My daughter, I see more Pharisees among the Christians than there were around Pilate. They renew My body's wounds so that, if that body were as large as the world, there would not be a spot the size of the point of a needle which would not be lacerated by their crimes. More Pharisees crucify Me to-day than at the time of My Passion."

This terrible lamentation continued, leaving Margaret so overwhelmed that Christ suddenly took pity on her: "You have anointed My wounds with your tears and have taken Me down from the cross."

If Margaret's meditation was such on Easter, what must it have been on the anniversary of Christ's death? We might be tempted to doubt the words of Brother Bevegnati, but he told only what he had seen. One Holy Thursday, Margaret, in an extremity of suffering, left her cell and, drunk with grief, her head shaven, she ran out into the street shrieking. In this condition she arrived at the Minorite

church. Out of fear of the brothers, she did not
dare repeat the same scene in all the churches.

People did not cry out that a lunatic was
loose. The personal destiny of so singular a
creature could flower in the town of Cortona.
The Shulamite ran into the street looking for
his Beloved and nobody found fault with him.
The Canticle of Canticles rang through the
town. But if the Beloved was perhaps black—
nigra sum sed formosa—since she had smeared
herself with soot, she no longer seemed so
charming as she of the sacred book; her head
was cropped and covered with ashes. The ravishing creature had just relived in her own flesh
all the tortures of the Passion. She emerged
disfigured from an ocean of grief. Yet this
living flame too could have sung, "I will rise
and go about the city. In the streets and broad
ways, I will seek Him Whom my soul loveth.
I sought Him, and I found Him not: *per vicos
et plateas quaerem quem diligit anima mea:
quaesivi illum et non inveni.*"

CHAPTER XVIII

The Judgment of Saint John
of the Cross

FOR THOSE WHO FIND THESE EXCESSES DISCON-
certing, let us again remember that other saints
have suppressed this wish for a sensible mani-
festation of the Lord. Saint John of the Cross
would not have permitted a penitent to be so
insatiable that he could not live without the
consolation of divine visits.

Perhaps he would have disapproved of this
prayer of Margaret: "Where now is the joy
of your presence which I seek above everything?" John of the Cross was fearful of the
beauty increate beyond all language, beyond
all vision. He expressly condemned people who
made divine words out of what they heard in
prayers. And he even mocked them: " *'God told*

me, God replied to me,' they assert, and yet most often they are talking to themselves."

The saint has written "most often"; therefore, he does not condemn them all. Moreover, in *The Ascent of Mount Carmel* (Book II, Chapter 31) he carefully describes the words he calls substantial, which he distinguishes from successive and formal words, in that they stamp their meaning upon the soul, "As would happen if, for example, Our Lord said to the soul, 'Love Me,' and at the same moment it had within itself and felt within itself the substance of love."

Indeed, that is what the words heard by Margaret of Cortona seemed to be. But would not John of the Cross have considered the wild exigency of our saint a dangerous temptation? He would certainly not have turned her away from the contemplation of Christ in His humanity, but he would have wanted her not to linger too long.

And certainly not everything is love in this anguished fervor which made Margaret sigh for a Christ visibly present; the truth is that she needed to be assured; in spite of so many favors, her terror was not yet overcome. One day, in order to restore her confidence, she needed no less in her ecstasy than to see the Virgin ask Christ to agree to hasten Margaret's entrance into heaven. On coming back to herself, the Saint again found peace; but, like Saint Theresa, she died of not dying.

Then she made an oath not to ask to be consoled any more. Doubtless she also became more secretive, and when she meditated on the Passion she forced herself to hide her grief. But the inner voice reproved her for this: "It was formerly your practice to show by your tears the pain you felt for My Passion; now, the fear of what others say, the fear of seeming to seek vainglory, impose silence on you. Continue to weep at My feet. Do not hold back your grief, do not hide it."

What would Saint John of the Cross have answered to a penitent who would have opposed him with such orders received from the Lord Himself? And yet nothing is less incredible than Christ's wish that a poor woman manifest before the people the mystery of a crucified God. A penitent must be a living preaching of the Cross before she dies, like Margaret, or after she has left the world, like Theresa of the Child Jesus; those faithful lamps have not shone to be put under a bushel. The great solitary eagles, a John of the Cross, soar far above the crowd and draw other chosen eagles in their wake. But God hides in the midst of cities, according to the needs of each age, among less sublime creatures who love, suffer, and expiate close to the ground, at man's height. And finally, the humblest rejoin the most sublime in the same nudity, in the same joy.

Nevertheless, what would the feverish Margaret have thought of the answer which Saint John of the Cross gave to a Carmelite: "My daughter, I always bear my soul within the Holy Trinity, and it is there that my Lord Jesus Christ wants me to bear it."

It was there too, near her Lord—no longer grasped in His visible humanity, but at the very center of the divine essence—that this Magdalene, whose fervor was unconsolable, appeased her anguish and stilled her cries. John of the Cross would have cured her of her excessive austerities, leading her, by a route where they

lose their significance, to the thickest part of
that dark night which is "the loss of taste in
the appetite for all things," all things, the spiritual as well as the sensible. To divest one's self
of everything which is not God means to renounce all devotion which interests the flesh, it
goes without saying, and even the heart; it is
to agree to fear God only in the pure darkness
of Faith.

One Pentecost day Margaret was astonished at not having received a personal sign of
grace and complained. "To the contrary," the
Lord replied to her, "I say to you that you have
received a very great sign of grace, but you
have not noticed it." Without meaning to do
so, Brother Bevegnati doubtless here states an
exhortation of Christ not to confuse grace with
the movements of sensibility.

Another day the Lord said to her, "You
constantly wish to draw the sweetness at the
sources of My heart, whereas I have received
so much bitterness from you. You always want
to be filled and satisfied when I have stayed
famished for your salvation." Again, "Fear
not, My daughter; if you do not taste the con-

solations you desire, yet, when in tears you call
Me, I stay with you. . . . But you always want
to be filled with My presence."

Another inspiration was very soon to be
given to Margaret to cure her of this avidity;
a dwelling was going to be shown to her in a
dream, the cell at the foot of the citadel where
Christ wanted her; and to attain it she was to
exhaust herself in crucifying debates. That
other cell, more solitary, higher, that last sta-
tion, at the extreme edge of the abyss, was also
the image of another prayer, of a more austere
contemplation—the selfsame one which leads
the soul to the unimaginable union. But first
she had to pass over dark and narrow paths.

CHAPTER XIX

The Martyrdom
of the Curious Beast

AT THE THRESHOLD OF THE LAST JOY, SHE HAD
to go through a hell which she had not foreseen.
The harshest disciplines, the most rigorous
facts are nothing to the ordeals which men in-
vent for us; there are no true torments except
those we have not chosen.

One day Christ warned Margaret, "Be
strong. Take courage. Grace will increase with
your pains. Tell your confessor to notify
Brother John (of Castiglione) to pray earnestly
for you, for your pains will be such that both
of them will have doubts about you, and those
doubts will remain fixed in the minds of some
people to the moment of your death."

He told her again, "You will suffer very

great pains. Cut off from all spiritual comfort,
remember at such a time what your confessor
told you, that when you were most thirsty for
Me, I was in your heart."

One day, while in an ecstasy, she received
this threat: "You would like to be the child of
sweetness, but will be the child of gall." At a
later time, already a refugee in her last cell, herself, stupefied at what she was going through,
Christ was to remind her, "Had I not warned
you that you would be suckled at My heart's
wound?"

The ordeals which were to burst over Margaret were to come almost entirely from this
notoriety, this great to-do about her ecstasy.
Would she have endured it if she had not
gathered such wonderful fruits from it? But
penitents besieged the confessional of Brother
Bevegnati who begged to be let alone. "Your
confessor charges you with sending very many
men and women to confess to him, people who
are led back to Me by your tears and prayers;
and he sends them away, claiming that he can
not clean so many stables in a single day!"
These souls deserved Margaret's being sacri-

ficed to the crowd; but every love seeks silence, secrecy. A soul which Christ had wounded would, more than any other, require solitude, were it not that it remembered that its God had been crucified naked before all the people. Those who identify themselves with Him must endure the humiliation of being exposed and sacrificed to all comers.

But it was not only friends who went in and out of the cell, the chapel in which Margaret's ecstasy resembled an agony. Doubtless, "poor little ones" from the hospital, the Moscari family, holy women, and the brothers surrounded her; but also the curious, the jealous, the ill-intentioned who only later were to show their true colors. On all calvaries, around all crosses, men wag their heads, shrug their shoulders, and taste the joy of outraging the victim.

After having suffered, second by second, the horrors of the Passion, Margaret opened her eyes; she found herself in the chapel of the Brothers without remembering having gone there. A crowd of people in tears was watching her. Having seen her suffer the same tortures as the Lord, they also thought that she was going to die His death. Sneering was already mixed with the sighs of the people. Crowds in the middle ages were no different from those of to-day; at Lourdes the host goes into the midst of people who are on their knees and sick people who are lying stretched out, but the scoffers look on from a distance.

On coming out of this hell, Margaret lost control of her actions and questioned the witnesses of her terrifying ecstasy. "Unfortunate one that I am, where shall I go?" she cried. "Where shall I find Him? Oh, if I could see You, with what infinite joy You would fill me! I seek, I sigh, I cry out, I keep watch, I take pains, because the cruellest death has snatched You from my love. Oh, angels, men, all of you, creatures, tell me: where is my crucified God? Alas, what have I done, Lord, that infinite kindness treats me so cruelly? My love, why have You abandoned me? Where are You hidden? I want to see and hear You. . . . Oh, unhappy one that I am, why live?"

She remained this way, without sleep, without food, consumed with anguish, until the following Sunday. And again on that day, she made a spectacle of herself, interrupting the sermon of the good brother with the eternal plaint of Mary Magdalene, "They have taken away my Lord; and I know not where they have laid Him."

In his account the brother humbly admits that he could not have made flow a single one of the tears that streamed down all the faces around Margaret. But more than one of those present said to himself within his heart, "It's a poor mad woman." Some who had believed in her began to doubt that it could end otherwise than in a lunatic asylum.

It was to the interest of some people to spread this opinion. Margaret had made enemies among those greedy devotees who had forced themselves upon her. A public saint belongs to all. She was watched over, spied on, for fear lest she run away, lest she go to die in a rival town and her body fall into strange hands. A saint's body does not inspire spiritual grace only. The least important Cortonian felt that he had rights over Margaret.

CHAPTER XX

The Saint Is Given to the Devotees

FROM THE TOP OF THE CROSS FROM WHICH
she hung with her Lord, Margaret heard these
questions with distaste; she entered these disputes reluctantly. For they were raising a fuss
about her as at the entrance of a circus or
around a public torture; the same kind of people
who would give their right arm for the pleasure
of seeing a torture or an execution.

One day a woman, annoyed that the neigh-
bors were freely entering the saint's cell, decided to keep guard and maintain order there.
We know this type of self-important person
who barks along the Catholic roads, those rear-
guard devotees, those hangers-on; their race
has not died out. So this woman tried hard to
drive away the good souls who were buzzing
around the saint. But one of the women took
this very ill and soon the two came to blows.

Snatched from her ecstatic contemplation by the brawling of the two old gossips, Margaret gently invited the one who wanted to enter to pass the night at her side, and tried to dismiss the too zealous guardian whose fury was immediately turned against Margaret. Brother Bevegnati does not tell us of the insults she had to submit to; but there can be no doubt that the raging woman then remembered the transgressions which had been so often bewailed in public and that she alluded to the murdered lover and to the bastard. . . . To put a stop to this flood of slime, the saint decided to spend a night out of her cell at the side of this shrew and humbly begged her to make a place for her in her house. Far from being touched by this, the fury refused to admit her.

The evil-minded persons who were waiting their chance had an opportunity to show themselves with a will. Margaret, who deprived herself of everything, could not do without a servant. Her body, enfeebled by penitence, was also broken by ecstasy; for it was the vessel of her own body that Magdalene had smashed at the feet of God.

This physical misery of the saints is really a misery in the eyes of Christians. It is not because of their weaknesses, but in spite of their weaknesses that they are saints. The breath of God burns the imprudent creature who comes too close.

Because she was dedicated solely to penance and had no other mission than to follow in the footsteps of her Master, how could she help being enfeebled, more so than any other saint, by the torture which was to end only in death. The woman who helped her, to whom she had devoted herself, took advantage of her and abused her confidence.

She had been assigned to go from house to house to collect in a small glass phial the bit of wine that Margaret had been ordered to drink. She had been told never to present herself more than once a month in any one house. But the servant was most careful not to obey; provided with an extremely large bottle, she often dropped in on the people who had shown themselves generous, and paid them with tales whose cost Margaret had to bear.

That was all that was necessary for people

to start having doubts. It was in vain that
Brother Bevegnati discharged the brazen woman; the scandal had been great. After all,
where did this Margaret come from? She was
returning, if not to her first loves, at least to
certain excesses which did not worry her in the
old days at Montepulciano, and which her
bodily weakness now excused. Certain scenes
which simple-minded people took for manifesta-
tions of grace, might well be the exploits of a
person who drank.

Even those who remained faithful were
secretly shaken. Some of the brothers, perhaps
Brother Giunta Bevegnati himself, began to be
less sure of her holiness. They still believed in
her since they refused to allow her to retreat
to the little cell at the foot of the mountain
which she had seen in a dream, fearing lest she
die outside of their supervision and take her
precious remains elsewhere. But they asked
themselves questions about her. Was there not
something diabolical in the affair?

Thus, Margaret began the unknown ordeal,
the one we do not choose and which men choose
for us. It is the experience of the Saints that it

is not enough to want to be crucified with Christ, and that the choice of the particular cross which is destined for us is not left in our own hands.

In every holy life, and even in every Christian life, despite the many crosses sought out or submitted to, there is only one *true* cross, one alone which counts, one which is not revealed to us at first. Sometimes, it does not unmask itself until rather late; it is necessary to have passed beyond the dark storm of youth for it to reveal itself. Little by little it emerges from the mists of passion. Suddenly it is there, like something we dared not name. It remains for us to stretch out upon it with love.

CHAPTER XXI

The Impossible Adaptation
to the World

THE TUMULT IN THE SAINT'S CELL, THE PRAT-
ing and bibulous servant, the petty scandals
provoked by the ecstasies, all of this, though it
seems hardly avoidable, gives the feeling of the
tragic unadaptability of the contemplative life
to the requirements of the world. And that
which is glaringly evident to one who experiences ecstasy is, to a lesser degree, true for
every man if he takes the Christian life seri-
ously—and for all the Holy Catholic Church.
Let revealed truth contradict the world, let it
take root there and endure only by virtue of
evasions, concessions, a diminution—this is,
when one thinks about it, rather decisive evidence.

The Gospel proclaimed that the time was close. The first Christian generation awaited the Lord's return from one day to the next, scanned heaven and earth for signs announcing the second coming. Christ's law struck head-on against a world which was condemned and about to disappear. The Christian virtues, poverty, chastity, obedience, glorified what it hated most. Without blinking an eye, the faithful renounced a criminal century whose destruction they were going to see, and, in their minds, they were already dwelling in the kingdom which is not of this world.

They are dead. More numerous than the sands of the sea, the generations have passed, and we, in our turn, are the first Christians awaiting the second coming. The only statement on this matter which has not deceived us is that of Saint Peter, in an epistle, when he reminds us that for God one day is as a thousand years and a thousand years as one day.

Since that time the Church has had to establish herself in time, she who was born for the end of time. How this decline drags out, at least if we measure it by the ephemeral duration of a human generation! The Church is holy and a Christian is holy only in the face of wind and tide. Their holiness is in proportion to the scorn with which the material conditions of their establishment here below inspire them. The more the saints conform to Christ, the more do they seem to us like creatures cast off from the simple and normal life, misfits, dying or not dying.

The enemies (secret or avowed) of Christ and his warmest friends fall into agreement. Pierre Bayle, commenting on Pascal, approves of his believing that there are almost no real Christians, which means that in his eyes pure Christianity is impracticable. And doubtless Saint Cyran is heretical; and I know quite well everything which it is permissible for us to find reassuring in certain formulas such as "to possess as if not possessing." Of course! Despite the maledictions of Christ, even the rich may be saved, and Saint Francis de Sales introduced Philotases of the court and the world to the holy life and even initiated them to pure love. But we must believe that they came to it only by means of an uprooting which was less spectacular but perhaps just as cruel as that which frightens us in our Margaret.

The truth is that from his first effort toward perfection, the Christian is unfaithful to his human interest, renounces "the delicious and criminal way of the world." This epitome of Pascal is Jansenist in appearance only. For a soul whom love has touched, there is nothing more in the world nor itself which at all stirs up one of the three lusts denounced by Saint John: *libido sciendi, libido sentiendi, libido dominandi.*

In the self-flaying which the humble Margaret of Cortona persisted in with sobs and screams and which her Italian mimicry makes glaringly evident, the cultivated saints, those versed in philosophy and letters display a violence which is less instinctive but just as terrible in its effects. Of course, even an ordinary Christian soon sets about finding his cross and he does not have to go far to seek it. But there is more than one way of clasping it; the saints stretch themselves out naked on it. By doing that Margaret resembles all her brothers and sisters in Christ. Only the saints are capable

of the final twitch at the garment which sticks
to our secret wound. We shall die in the Lord,
if He so wishes, yes, we hope so, we ordinary
Christians. But we shall die still wrapped in a
final pride, a final ambition, a not quite smothered tenderness. Holiness is nudity.

CHAPTER XXII

Holiness, Source of All Joy

AND YET, THIS OPPOSITION BETWEEN THE CROSS
and the "simple and normal" life exists only
in our lust; it does not appear in reality. The
cross opposes the voluptuous, triumphant life,
as we dream it to be, as we think we taste it at
certain times, but the cross is not opposed to life
as it is. The saints do not introduce the cross to
their destiny; they find it there all set up. Instead of diverting themselves from it, in the
Pascalian sense, by pleasures and games, or,
fleeing it through the thousand loopholes which
men have discovered (from tobacco and alcohol to drugs and all the disguised forms of
suicide) they question it, they snatch its secret
of love and joy. We are free to believe that they
give in to a comforting illusion, but not that
they add a worse horror to the human condition

than it already allows, for the deniers of the cross, the worshippers of pleasure are not less crucified than the saints.

The latter have never believed that sadness was a good in itself. They know that it is the evil attached to the original sin. Neither do they deny that human life, especially in its beginnings, knows serene hours nor that happy hours are given to the most unhappy. They themselves have often tasted its delights.

"Farewell to the gaiety of my youth, to careless folly, to the free and joyous life at the foot of Vesuvius! Farewell to gay meals, to evening chats, to serenades beneath the gilded balconies! Farewell to Naples and its women, to masquerades by torchlight, to long suppers in the forest shadows. Farewell to love and friendship."

The young Francis, prince of the youth of Assisi would not have been at all shocked by this farewell to the sweetness of living that the romantic Octave gives vent to in *Marianne's Whims*. For Francis of Assisi, and our Margaret too, knew wild masqerades, passions of the heart, the tenderness of an enchanted heart.

Perhaps they even attached more importance to these earthly joys than we ourselves do because they were destined for sainthood. Everything that can be said about the days that follow drunkenness, about the nothingness of pleasure, about death and sickness which prowl about, about the intermittent character of human love, its fierceness, its betrayals, its impurities, nothing in all that has diverted them from being mindful of the meaning of that hunger and thirst for happiness, for happiness through the love which they reveal in us. They know that there are infinite moments in the most wretched attachments. Human art in its finest flower gives us this same lesson. Mozart reveals to those who love him the mystery of a ravishing happiness, quite near and, at the same time, inaccessible. The Saints who began by sinning were mistaken in the object of their desire. They do not deny this desire of their heart, but in order to crush it they have learned to substitute being for nothingness.

The way of the cross in which they are involved, the suffering which they seek, which they provoke, they do not seek it for its own

sake. It is a route—foreshortened—toward the
object of their adoration. And since they knew,
as Saint John of the Cross has written, that
what is born of the world is the world, and
what is born of the flesh is the flesh, and that
therefore "God never communicates Himself
either by the world or by the flesh," they mortify in themselves the sensual tastes, the appe-
tites. This deprivation alone brings them close
to a beloved One Who is beyond the body,
beyond beings, Who awaits them beyond all
passion and all desire. These eccentrics are, in
their suffering, infatuated with joy. How can
they help pitilessly immolating that which sepa-
rates them from that joy?

No one except the saints is happy. "Joy!
Joy! Tears of joy!" cried Pascal. There is not
one of them who, amidst the torments of a
consumed life, has not felt this cry rise from
his heart to his lips. And at certain hours even
the most miserable, the most empty-handed,
the least crucified Christian, one who, in a whole
lifetime of impurities can boast of nothing more
than a meagre fidelity, has known these tears of
joy.

Despite her martyrdom, our Margaret never stopped exulting thus in God her Lord. "Oh, Father!" she cried. "My Resurrection and my Life, my Spouse, my Joy, Oh, Life of my life!" Her confessor assures us that in the course of a certain ecstasy she was flooded with such happiness that she thought her heart would burst. One night (it was Saint Claire's Day) an angel fluttered above her cell. As he was blessing her, "she suddenly felt herself inflamed with so ardent a love that not being able to contain her inner joy, she let herself be flooded. . . . As I begged her to explain to me the strangeness of this joy, she told me that it was the privilege of this seraph to inflame hearts with an unspeakably joyous love."

This "strange joy" is the common patrimony of the friends of Jesus Christ. How jubilant a symphony might be composed by uniting the texts which testify to this unimaginable happiness, from the cry of Stephen, the first martyr, whose face was that of an angel, to the exaltations of an Augustine, to the marvelous prayer of Saint Gertrude to her "evening Jesus," to the cries of the Catherines, the

Theresas, to the Canticle of John of the Cross, to the stammerings of our Mary of the Incarnation! "You are called fire. No, my love, You are not fire, You are not water, You are nothing that we say. You are what You are in Your glorious eternity. You are!"

At times the ordinary Christian gets irritated. Who has ever loved so? Who has ever experienced this kind of love? What balanced and wise mind could conceive this inhuman love?

The truth is that this love is hardly ever spoken about. Human passion is celebrated, analyzed, exalted in books, in music, in painting. Over the radio innumerable romances keep the cult going from dawn to dusk. There is an unbelievable disproportion between what men hear said of love and what they experience of it in their poor lifetime.

Divine love is silent. Humble hearts do not betray their secret, knowing that they would not be understood by men. It is an incommunicable charm. To confide this marvel to others would be to destroy it.

God allows it to be betrayed sometimes in

a cry. Sometimes by chance a paper is found
on which a man has scrawled for himself alone
that which exceeds human language; it is the
Memorial of Pascal, or again, the *Mystery of
Jesus* whose every word still scorches us.

If all those who have reasons for under-
standing what it is that intoxicates the mystics
could speak, it would be apparent that this love
of God is offered to many more creatures than
one imagines. "Perhaps," the adversary insinuates, "but it's always the same kind of person;
everything happens as if one did or did not have
the disposition for the devotional life; just as
some people have a gift for languages, others
have a gift for God."

It is true that some men are born lovers as
others are born mystics; moreover, there exists
no abyss between these two vocations. Many,
especially among women, pass from one to the
other. What Madame de Sévigné said about
Jean Racine, that he loved God as he had loved
his mistresses, is confirmed in many destinies.
How wonderful a love of God it has been given
us to know in some aged women who remain
marked by the terrible fire, their faces hollowed

out by all the tears of a tormented life. And now it was the tears of a holy joy which streamed down, covering the traces of the old lava.

CHAPTER XXIII

Abandoned by Men
and the Father

IN THE OCTAVE OF SAINT FRANCIS THE LORD
once again announced to Margaret that certain
Minorites would break away from her: "You
will be darkness for the eyes of light." And He
added, "Those who think you are in the darkness will know you after death, to their great
shame."

But for Margaret this ordeal at the hands of
the Minorites was to be nothing compared to
the other desertion; it is the supreme ordeal of
the saints, the one which, more surely than
consumption, was the death of little Thérèse of
Lisieux, the hell which none of these consumed
souls has been spared. The Master disclosed it
to His servant in advance: "I shall and shall

not be with you. I shall clothe you in My Grace, but you will think yourself deprived of it, because while dwelling within you, I shall be able to go unrecognized."

He did not conceal His plan to introduce her to a loftier state: "You have passed beyond the first degrees by which one arrives at grace. I want you to mount higher in knowledge of Me. Just as I concealed My power on the cross, I am concealing Myself from you so that you may discover by yourself what you are without Me."

He was to take her as far as a creature can advance without dying—to the threshold where nothing more remained for her but to pass to eternal life: "Daughter, whose charity is exposed to so much discontent and who will be crowned in Heaven (since you have felt more for the shedding of My blood than has any other creature, and since nobody has bewept My death as much as you,) daughter, I have known tribulation, you too will be afflicted. I have known a dejection that you too will bear. They whispered against Me, you will suffer the same whispers. Now I am in glory, you too will one day be raised to it. But I say to you again: your suffering will double."

So, having predicted to her all that she was to suffer, He showed her the same path as the great mystics had followed before the last delights of the transforming union: "Daughter of tribulation, of glory, and of grandeur, your heart will know such turmoil that not only will you think yourself far from the stage of grace which I have promised you, but you will even think yourself fallen from the one you had attained."

On the first of May, 1288, Margaret preferring to obey God rather than men, finally escaped from the curious and sometimes malicious crowd. Against the advice of the Minorites, she secluded herself in the poor hovel on Mount Sant-Egidio near the ruined church of Saint Basil (or of Saint Egidio) which had been built in the past by the monks of the Order of Saint Romuald. The Arezzians had destroyed it in 1258. The township of Cortona permitted Margaret to dispose of it provided that Guglielmo Ubertini, bishop of Arezzo, agreed. This prelate, a sort of petty condottiere,

neglected to answer the saint and in the mean-
time was killed at the battle of Campaldino.
After two years of waiting, his successor, Hil-
debrand, finally gave in. But the Minorites allowed Brother Giunta Bevegnati henceforth to
visit Margaret only once a week.

Don Badia Ventura, chaplain of the re-
stored church, substituted for him at the side
of his penitent. Following an order of Christ,
Margaret had an altar set up in the cell; God
covered it with a particular benediction: "For
love of you, new light, I bless the cell where you
live concealed for My love."

The new warden, Giovanni of Castiglione,
whom the Chapter of Siena had elected in 1288,
without being a declared opponent of Margaret, decided to put her under observation.
Brother Bevegnati himself had let himself
yield to doubt and Margaret had the grief of
seeing her spiritual father pass over to the
enemy. Moreover he does not deny it but piously
vents himself against the demon: "The serpent,
he whose role it is to try the elect, who always
lays his snares, did not forget the threat he
made concerning me. He tried to set my mind

against that daughter of God, the more so because I thought her indiscreet in embracing so austere a life. He suggested that I stop visiting her for a while. (Does this mean, then, that he abandoned Margaret voluntarily and not at the order of the warden?) She, without ever departing from her gentleness, did not stop praying to Our Lord on my behalf."

To tell the truth, the good brother seems rather to have joined the pack of wolves. It must be acknowledged that Margaret's excesses confused human wisdom: "Seeing that sorry state of her emaciated body, wasted with fasting, tears, discipline, the hair-cloth, and all sorts of infirmities, I feared lest she succumb very shortly." This confidence betrays the confessor's terrible perplexities.

The distrust of the Minorites increased, but without ever becoming outright hostility. John of Castiglione died in 1290 and was succeeded by Brother Philip who at once took a radical step. He exiled Brother Bevegnati to the convent of Siena where Margaret's confessor stayed for seven years. Thus did the penitent enter the night as had been foretold. The Fran-

ciscan soul, no longer of this world, except
through its attachment to the Order, was now
suspect if not rejected, officially branded, in a
way, with a sign of mistrust by the very ones to
whom Christ had confided it. One of the women
who had been most occupied with her (perhaps
one of the Moscaris) even went so far as to ac-
cuse her of frivolity. The Lord ordered Margaret to speak to nobody about this woman's
contempt.

There is a Christian drama of obedience.
How can it be denied that the answer of all
the martyrs that it is better to obey God than
man opens the door to all the aberrations of
proper meaning? For if it is true that God
sometimes speaks directly to a soul, its good
faith does not preserve it from the danger of
illusion, since it is itself the only witness. "Tell
your confessor from Me," Christ repeated to
Margaret, "not to divert you from the cell near
the rock, to write to Brother John that this
change does not warrant his withdrawing his
solicitude for you." But at the very moment
that Brother Giunta was receiving this counsel
from Margaret he had been won over by doubt

concerning the inner words which she had reported to him. If she felt some bitterness about this, none of it appeared in the letter she wrote him when he was at the convent of Siena, a letter which he has preserved for us.

Abandoned by men, Margaret thought she was also abandoned by God, because the imitation of Christ should extend to the cry of the crucified Son, "My God, my God, why hast Thou forsaken me?" But Brother Giunta does not linger over that night that Margaret went through, when God was attained by virtue of a denuding, a despoiling of everything—even of the sacred joys which came from Him and yet which were not He—never so near a soul as when He pretends to have deserted it, never closer to absorbing it, to transforming it into Himself than when He manages to despoil it, to empty it of itself.

Margaret had to face and conquer the revolt of nature against this pitiless master, against this God "Who loves so much the bodies which suffer," as Pascal says of Him. We shall see that like all her brothers and sisters in holiness, she knew the demon; not as we ourselves know

him, by mere suggestions (in such a case he is
hardly distinguished from our vices), but she
knew him substantially. She saw him face to
face, and never so formidable as when he pitied
her: "Oh, unhappiest woman in the world," he
whispered to her. "What is your Master? To
Whom have you enchained your heart with so
singular and exclusive a love? He Whom you
love, this Jesus Whom you seek night and day
and for Whom you crucify your flesh with all
sorts of tortures, is so cruel an idol that He
gives His love only to those who give up everything and destroy themselves for Him."

Cruel idol: the fearful words were pro-
nounced—doubtless in one of those nocturnal
moments when the soul no longer apprehends
God except through the darkness of Faith,
when with all the power of its will, it believes
in that love of which nothing is any longer evident. No creature had surpassed Margaret in
the mortification of the senses, but doubtless
there still remained a good deal for her to know
about the second mortification of spiritual delights and inner comforts. She was not entirely
unfamiliar with the evil which John of the

Cross denounced when he spoke of souls which seek God but which "abhor like death harshness, aridity, inner pains, and poverty of spirit, and seek, on the contrary, the more gentle of God's communications, spiritual satiety, which can hardly be called abnegation or nakedness of spirit, but rather spiritual gluttony."

Certainly Margaret had already mortified in herself this sublime sensuality of the saints; but overwhelmed by remorse over her youth, she still sought the pleasures of devotion, which were palpable to the senses, less for their joys than for the sign which she recognized of her return to grace. Crushed as she was, her humility did not go so far as to grow satisfied with itself. Her immense love sought not comfort but certainty. It needed reassurance. Without any doubt, it was in regard to this that God's silence became such a terrible ordeal for this anxious soul: "What if He has departed? What if the weight of my sins has finally been too much for Him?"

The memory of the penance which she had inflicted upon herself for so many years no longer helped her, for the enemy used it against her: "You really ought to know," he hinted, "that you're never going to receive God's pardon for your sins—which you never stop asking for—because you've killed yourself with your abstinence."

Saint John of the Cross points out that in that night of the spirit which follows the night of the senses the greatest torture of the soul is believing that it is hated by God. Margaret forgot about the work that love had achieved in her. She no longer felt like clay in the potter's hands. Spiritually despoiled, as for years she had been carnally, this harshness of God's lent her none of the supports which had formerly helped her among men. Completely detached from both God and the world, a creature rejected everywhere, she had no presentiment of the approach of the supreme joy. On the contrary, the memory of former felicities pierced her heart.

But even if Brother Giunta Bevegnati had not abandoned her, the help she would have received from him would have been no more efficacious than that of Don Badia who had replaced him at her side. What would they have

understood of this strange misery? According
to Saint John of the Cross, the soul in this
state "resembles a man in a dark prison whose
hands and feet are kept bound. He can neither
move nor see anything nor get the slightest re-
lief. In like manner the soul in the darkness
groans under its chains, motionless, helpless,
until the spirit is softened, humbled, purified,
so subtle, so simple, that it can, in some way,
become one with the spirit of God, in accordance with the extent and degree of the union of
love to which mercy wishes to raise it."

Step by step Margaret followed this exhausting itinerary which John of the Cross was
to describe two centuries later: "The souls
which suffer from such an affliction love God
even unto giving a thousand lives for Him. But
this great love does not keep them from believing that they are not loved, since they find in
themselves nothing worthy of that love and
even consider themselves wretched enough to
deserve the hatred of God and the horror of
His creatures (*The Dark Night,* II, 7)."

CHAPTER XXIV

Christ's Pity
for His Crucified Servant

ONE WOULD SOMETIMES THINK THAT CHRIST could no longer stand seeing His servant suffer and that He might let fall the word which would rescue her: "Set your mind at rest, you will not be deceived, you are written in the book of life."

One muses on the sublime litanies that might be composed in honor of Margaret using nothing but the wonderful names given to her by her Lord and her God by Whom she was so foolish as to think herself unloved! "Daughter of gall—daughter whose charity is exposed to grumbling—daughter of tribulation, glory, and grandeur—daughter of perfect faith—star— My chosen one, My companion, My sister—

Margaret, My martyr—living sanctuary of My grace—rose, white for innocence, rose, red for love."

This torturing God never left her without consolation. When the ordeal was hardest, He suddenly became a great calm in her; the Christ Who was asleep at the stern had awakened.

Then came the hour when the Lord wished to uproot this frightful doubt of a penitent who thought herself unworthy of pardon. How many other saints have tasted the grace of being pardoned by Christ Himself? The unimaginable joy of hearing addressed to one's self the same words that the halt and the blind heard, "Thy sins are forgiven thee," and by the same mouth—this joy Margaret knew. A hand was raised above her brow, the same beneath which the ruined woman, the toll-collector, had bowed.

"Confess to your Lord, My daughter." This invitation came to her one day when everything that she had done since she had begun to sin was present to her thought and her grief brought her to the point of fainting. Then she begged her Judge not to spare her and wished that death alone might interrupt so terrible a suffering, one with no consolation. But He spread out His hand over her who had understood to the letter the order not to follow Christ unless with her cross. And suddenly she was released: "My daughter, I absolve you in the name of the Father, in My name, and in the name of the Holy Ghost, of all sins of thought, word, and action which you have committed up to this day."

Perhaps it was not the Master's will that Margaret undergo such torture, since He here strove to free her from it. But freedom of the soul runs risks for good as well as evil, for excess of penance as well as for guilty pleasures. Margaret resisted the grace of appeasement which Christ lavished on her. To what point did He not go in his tenderness toward the penitent martyr. But wind and sea obey Him because they are not soul. Even in a very holy soul the infinite Being strikes against a willfulness which disarms it. Margaret did not want the great calm which subdued the waves of the Lake of Tiberias. She was a bird of foam and storm. She felt her love only at the far edge of despair.

To measure the happiness of being pardoned, of being assured of it—and not only hoping, like the ordinary Christian—one has to be a sinner and a Christian; one must have a knowledge of sin, experience that persons of a pure life can possess—if they are Christ's—while base creatures know it not because they have lost the perception of evil; to feel one's self soiled and rejected by God is already a very great state of Grace.

Far from awakening in us the sense of sin, the enormity of our faults, on the contrary, increases in people at the same time as they are purified. Anyone who knows he is a sinner is already converted. Who has not heard the words, "I have never done any evil?" And he who uttered them was a thief, an adulterer, a sodomite. At the first sign of shame, less than that—at the first doubt, at the first anxiety that a glance at himself awakens in a man who examines his life, we know that God is near.

If Christ requires a Margaret to love and suffer in the eyes of all, it is the vocation of saints to compel Christians to see how far horror of self can go in a soul dedicated to perfection. But to experience this horror, it is necessary to love. God alone gives us those movements of the heart that are always accompanied by repentance. The purer love becomes, the greater grows our grief at having offended the God we love. The grace of seeing one's self as it is, the grace of lucidity, is not obtained by human means. What the wretchedness of an honest and, by the world's lights, devoted life can be in the eyes of infinite Purity was revealed to Margaret of Cortona in a few words which hit at all of us Christians of the privileged classes.

CHAPTER XXV

The Eternal Bourgeoise

A WOMAN WHO BELONGED TO THE HIGHEST society of Cortona, a very pious woman, gave proof of so much devotion to Margaret that the saint prayed for her benefactress incessantly. One day Christ spoke to her about this soul. "My daughter," he told her, "tell your confessor about the shortcomings of her for whom you pray to Me so often. I shall tell you what they are one after the other so that your confessor may be able to tell her about them to her great gain." It is Christ Himself Who proposes this terrifyingly minute examination of conscience to so many perfect people who, every week, bring trifles to the confessional and glory in finding no sin in themselves.

"Tell her that she who is so devoted to you out of love for Me had, before her marriage, a heart of doubtful virtue. Let her confess having desired too passionately the man who is

now her husband and of having sought him
with immoderate desire. Let her confess this
false virtue in her looks, her words, her gestures. . . .

Let her confess that at the time when a misfortune occurred to one of her parents, she
gave false testimony and helped, as much as
was in her power to do so, to render the judge's
sentence unjust, and that she felt less grief for
the degrading record which the accused thereby
incurred than for the money which she made
him lose.

Let her reveal her offense against Me when
she betook herself to the Palace of the Podestat
to hear herself proclaimed the most beautiful
among her friends (already queens of beauty!).

Let her admit often having accused servants secretly to their masters, hoping to win
their friendship by an indiscreet zeal in med-
dling in their affairs, a zeal which was only
hypocrisy since she had no real affection either
for them or for anyone except her husband
and children whom she loved excessively.

Let her reveal her inordinate fondness for
delicate foods.

Let her bewail her hardness of heart toward
the poor.

Let her admit the use she has made of ill-
gotten gains. Let her remember everything she
has thus spent. How much money has she not
spent in this way, money pilfered from her
husband, money coming from frauds, money
extorted by violence, money won at gam-
bling. . . .

As the mother of a family, she was in
charge of household expenses; let her remember how many useless purchases she made, how
many superfluous things she bought with money
that was wrongly acquired. . . . (What rich
and pious woman ever asks herself questions
about 'those things which make one shudder,'
which Bourdaloue has denounced as being at
the source of every great fortune?).

Let her admit the jealousy that she har-
bored against her parents who did not support
her husband's quarrels, the proud domination
she exercised in her husband's family, she who
would never have allowed her sister-in-law to
behave so in her own. Let her admit her greed
in regard to her husband's wards whom she had

to take care of because they were poor. Let her remember all the injuries she directed against persons of the household in season and out, and with what pride she adorned her body. . . .

Let her confess the bad things she said and the rash judgments she made concerning the neighbor whose qualities she scorned and disparaged, recalling the faults that she knew about and concealing the good and finding the means of accusing him of other faults of which he was not guilty.

Let her confess the harsh disclosures she made about those who were absent and her flatteries before those who were present.

Let her admit her thirst for honor and praise, her desire to seem richer than others, her jealousy at the idea that others might be superior to her in wealth and beauty, her distraction at church in the presence of other women.

In spite of what I have done for her, I have been unable to attach Myself to her, and if at times she has served Me, it has been out of fear, not out of love.

Although she is free of the vice of impurity,

yet she has soiled the marriage bed. She has felt no repugnance at finding herself among those who offend Me in their flesh, she who is full of spiritual vices.

Let her admit how careful she has been to blame others, whether for their ill-gotten gains, their lands, the luxuriousness of their clothes and their perfumes, she who has sought the pleasures of good living and has given alms out of ostentation.

Let her confess her indiscretions concerning her servants, her rash judgments concerning the poor and how she scorned their pleadings, their tears, and their pleasures, their games, and their eating and drinking as well (this last trait is wonderful).

She denies herself nothing in what concerns the number and richness of her garments and does not worry herself at all about covering their nakedness nor appeasing their hunger.

Let her admit having usurped the name which befitted My Mother only when she had herself called Sovereign, she who ridiculed others when they assumed that name.

Although she has moved in the society of

the most beautiful and best dressed persons, she has always thought herself superior to them.

Let her admit the frivolity which brings her to exaggerate her sufferings, always regarding them as greater than those of others, she who remains cold and indifferent before their misfortunes.

Let her confess her harshness in regard to her servants to whom she gave no rest after hard work, whether they were ill or not. Instead of the comforting which they needed they received only insults and abuse and were accused of gluttony and negligence. As for herself, their mistress treated herself with high consideration, spoke when she should have kept quiet, and kept quiet when she should have spoken. Let her confess having avoided deformed persons. . . . In spite of all these faults let her have confidence in My mercy. Let her not delay going to her confessor. Yet I say unto you, Margaret, My daughter, that this woman whom you recommend so urgently to My mercy will not fully agree to these favors."

CHAPTER XXVI

Doubts About This Indictment

THIS INDICTMENT AGAINST THE WOMAN OF ALL times and of all countries continued, minute, captious.

But we turn away with a certain inquietude from the human interest that it raises in us; it was Christ Who spoke, it was from Christ's mouth that Margaret received this diatribe— or thought she did.

But we know how Jesus addresses Himself on the earth to the sinner, what words He uses when He speaks of the sinner. Every one of His statements which we retain, and those which have been transmitted with fervent scrupulousness, gives off a unique sound. We, His flock, are so familiar with His adored voice that our ear is sensitive to the slightest false note.

Even when He does not address public sin-

ners like the Samaritan, like the woman taken
in adultery, or Mary Magdalene, even when
He sees stretched out at His feet only the
paralytic or the man who has been born blind,
He does not withdraw His Godly scrutiny of
their lives for a single day.

But no! He is never lost in the labyrinth of
a human life. Whatever the creature He is considering, Jesus says to him, "Thy sins are forgiven thee," and all is swept clean, scattered,
annihilated, the trifle and the crime, the big and
the small—and that is why one need not be
scandalized at the apparent indifference of the
Catholic confessor to the faults that a penitent
whispers to him through the grill. The unfathomable mercy of which He is the incarnation devours all these impurities.

And here we are, caught up in doubt, as
was the good Brother Giunta Bevegnati himself. We too doubt Margaret. How could she
have believed that this too clearsighted diatribe
of a poor woman, unconsciously exasperated
by her benefactress, came to her from Jesus?
Without realizing it, she noted from day to day
everything that shocked and annoyed her in a

fine lady who was pious and pharisaical. The saint here yields to the woman; a woman observes another woman and avoids sinning against charity by attributing this merciless examination to her God.

But if Margaret duped herself this time, what guarantee have we that this was not always the case, that it was not she herself who was always talking to herself? An uneasiness running stealthily across this meditation on a saintly life, one which I can no longer brush aside. Moreover, is it my duty to brush it aside? Must a Christian, by definition, be a biased mind? The adversary would like to sow this doubt in us.

The Christian knows what truth is. And not only does he breathe and move in it, but he knows its name and its face. It has been revealed to him that it is Someone Who came into the world, Who manifested Himself to the world. Oddly enough, it happens that the consequence of his certainty of possessing it in its very essence, of drinking at its source, makes him less scrupulous in regard to partial truths. It matters little to him if such and such a tale is only a legend, if what it illustrates is true. If some of us yield uncritically to ill-founded credulities, it is because it never concerns anything but legends which are composed *within* the truth. Thus, some of the disciples who said to Pilate, "For this was I born, and for this came I into the world; that I should give testimony to the truth. Everyone that is of the truth heareth my voice," almost seem less sensitive to intellectual honesty than some of their opponents, thereby yielding, without thinking that they are doing wrong, to the euphoria of certainty.

Minds of this kind persuade themselves that the first religious virtue, faith, can manifest itself in no surer way than by unreflecting adherence to every phenomenon offered to them as supernatural. Contrariwise, they readily regard as suspect the priest or layman who, outside the truths of faith, scrupulously admits nothing without examination—the faith of a glutton to whom everything is good, the best and the worst. But is it meritorious in the eyes of the God of truth to believe that a certain apparition took place if it is the result of a half-concocted illusion of some children? We are no longer obliged to close our eyes to the difference in nature between the words of Christ reported by some person in an ecstasy and the words transmitted by the Evangelists. Pascal wrote, "Jesus Christ said great things so simply that it seems that He did not think them and, nevertheless, so clearly that one quite sees what He was thinking. The union of this clarity and naïveté is remarkable." The diatribe against the woman is remarkable also, but not naïve, and thereby one sees quite well that, at least, those words were human. But there remain many others which, despite Brother Giunta's dull prose (or that of his translator), we have no trouble in believing divine.

In Chapter XXV of *The Story of My Life* Saint Theresa of Avila assures us that the inner words carry their own certainty with them. This did not prevent her, according to the testimony of theologians who studied her case, from believing for two years, or forcing herself to believe, that the words which charmed her came from the demon. These wise men seem to have been unable to conceive the fact that the words were neither God's nor the Devil's but Theresa's herself.

As for Margaret, we must not lose sight of the state to which her penance reduced her. This was not the least important reason which induced Theresa of Avila and John of the Cross to put those entrusted to their direction on guard against the abuse of disciplines and the hair-cloth, that non-resistance of an enfeebled creature to illusion, nightmares, and mirages.

CHAPTER XXVII

Margaret and the Demon

MARGARET WAS SEEING SNAKES WHICH SHE took for bad angels: "He entered her cell in the guise of a frightful looking snake, and, fixing her with poison distilling stares, hissing horribly, his head raised in the air, he darted toward her with dazzling speed. . . . He was so long that only after the space of an hour . did she see all of him. So black was his malice that during this time the eyes of God's servant were clouded so that they could distinguish nothing. Not satisfied with appearing in this way while she was at prayer, he sometimes got on her bed, sometimes suspended himself along the wall, and then got down on the floor; sometimes, either on entering or leaving, he opened his mouth and hissed horribly, imitating the stamping and the roaring of a multitude."

Let us not be misunderstood; we are of those who believe that evil too is Someone (Someone who is multiple and whose name is legion)—moreover, of all the truths of Faith nothing disconcerts us more than this power given to an invisible enemy over the human creature who is already so unarmed and who is usually unaware of the fact that Satan exists. A disconcerting truth, but one which corresponds to certain experiences and is the key of certain destinies.

I doubt whether it has ever been possible to show scientific evidence of the Satanic presence in a life. One must first believe in the demon's existence in order to recognize it. But then, we can smell his presence a mile away!

Of course, not among all sinners. There is nothing demoniacal about many sinners. It is one thing to be in the realm of the demon, as we all are when we have lost the state of grace, and it is quite another to be held and surrounded, literally possessed by him.

This kind of possession does not betray itself by convulsions or grinding of teeth. Rather, it manifests itself in bodily vigor, sometimes by an angelic expression on the face, a great sharpness of intelligence, above all by a strange and constant happiness. That which should harm such a man does not at all hinder his success; on the contrary, it serves his vanity. Awful as his vice may be, he gratifies it easily and benefits from a wonderful abundance of opportunity without its costing him anything. What dishonors others serves him. He who has eternity to make amends will not pay his debt here below.

What one almost always finds at the heart of these careers is a clear choice, a refusal of God, a deliberate renunciation of His grace. So deliberate that the man recalls the period of his life when he agreed to it, and sometimes even the very day and hour when he said "no."

In the case of such a reprobate, all the elements of the saint he might have been almost always appear, and, at the height of his vilest corruption, one is amazed to discover in him faith in eternity, knowledge of the invisible world, an almost physical experience of the supernatural life.

And at the very same time that these creatures have (what is refused to most pious people) the certainty that everything which the church teaches is true, that they touch the most terrifying of these truths with their finger, it avails them nothing because they do not have love. They walk into the abyss with their eyes wide open.

No! he who has known the demon in man can never believe that he ever takes the form of a dragon or a hippogriff. Nothing resembles him less than those monsters begotten by the imagination of the penitent saint: "The apostle calls the demons princes because of the excellence of their nature." Thus does the catechism of the Council of Trent express itself.

It is not that Margaret had nothing to do with him, nor that we do not recognize him at her side; but the subtle doctor who harassed her was not one of those who disguise themselves as sea-serpents. He knew well enough that he would not penetrate this creature, who had been crucified with Christ, with such gross tricks. He went over the terrain, sought the weak spots, and it is amazing to see that he did not miss a single one of them.

André Gide, commenting on Dostoievski's notion of the demon, points out that the Russian novelist locates the devil "not at all in the base region of man but rather in the highest region, the intellectual region, that of the brain. The great temptations which the Fiend presents to us are, according to Dostoievski, temptations of the intellect, *questions*."

That is just the way it was with Margaret. First he exploited the doubt against which she was not always able to defend herself, about the origin of the words which intoxicated her. "It is not Christ nor an angel, but myself who have granted you the consolations which you think are due to Christ." He suggested to her only those thoughts whose germ Margaret already bore within her. He irritated a wound which had been tormenting her for a long time, as when he whispered to her, "Do you know that you are damned for not having been in harmony with the immense kindnesses which you have received from God, kindnesses which He will one day turn against you, and whose mistake you will expiate by eternal punishment?"

How can there be any doubt about the Enemy's attacking Margaret through her son. Brother Bevegnati tells us nothing about this matter, but it was the most vulnerable spot: "What have you done with that soul born of your lust and sacrificed to false saintliness? What have you made of that little creature on whom life was inflicted by criminal pleasures only to condemn him to child martyrdom? You have made a sullen novice of him who had inherited from his father the power of high birth, the taste for noble pleasures. You have turned him away from his native soil, from manly struggles, from kisses, from sleeping against a beloved bosom, but you have not opened paradise to him. Because these souls wandering between heaven and earth, rejected by both God and the world, are the share reserved for me; they are given to me. You consecrated this child to me, after a fashion, even before he was born. Do you not think that his grief which will never end, this eternal despair, is a high price to pay for your eternity of joy?"

It must have been then that Margaret, prostrated with her face against the floor, heard the

liberating words: "Your son will be saved."
Yes, saved with everything which was lost; for
"the Son of man is come to seek and to save
that which was lost."

But the enemy, driven off for a moment,
started crawling again, and little by little approached her until his breath burned her. He
knew where to strike her; he knew the scruples
by which, in spite of itself, a saintly soul is
consumed. For the road to perfection skirts the
abyss of despair. To the very end, despair remains the temptation of those who have not re-
treated in the face of Christ's command: "Be
you therefore perfect, as also your heavenly
father is perfect." "Be advised," he whispered
to her, "that because you have killed yourself
with your abstinences, you will never receive
from God the pardon for your sins that you
are constantly asking for."

Even when, in spite of himself, the fallen
angel betrayed his hatred of Christ; even when
he exhaled it in the furious adjuration we have
already cited, "He Whom you love, this Jesus
Whom you seek night and day and for Whom
you crucify your flesh with all sorts of tor-

ments, is so cruel an idol that He gives His love only to those who destroy themselves for Him," even when this outburst betrayed and unmasked him, he knew that he was awaking in Margaret a buried thought, whose existence was almost unknown to her, a doubt, an anxiety.

For she still owned a mirror . . . or had she perhaps seen her reflection in the windowpane? Well, well! This emaciated creature, dressed in rags or with a mat rolled around her, this shaven skull, this ruined face, this body overwhelmed with infirmities which she herself brought on—so that's the state to which Christ reduces His loved ones!

Margaret's immense love did not even allow this thought time enough to show its head, and she got over it before she even became conscious of it. But how can we doubt that the tempter did not then cast about and discover a more cautious and surer way to get at her? He no longer denounced the merciless Christ. On the contrary, he protested that the Son of God could not have desired the degradation of His creature, that Margaret was mistaken, that every page of the Gospels, every statement of

Christ, proved that she was the victim of an irreparable mistake. Did those who followed Him in Galilee have their faces smeared with soot? On the contrary, He commanded them to anoint their heads, especially when they were fasting. No one with a self-imposed infirmity came to Him, because those who bothered Him were there only so that He might heal them. His disciples sat down at the tables of the rich and of sinners.

Margaret must have answered, "Yes, because they had the Spouse with them; but when He left them, they began to suffer. And I have chosen my moment to unite myself with those who follow Him. It was not when the throng shook the branches and cried Hosanna. I mingled in the little band that followed after Him only when, having left the room where they had eaten the Passover dinner, they crossed the Cedron and went into the garden. I entered with Him into His agony. Second by second, I lived the last hours of His mortal life between the two agonies, the one of the sweating of blood in the darkness, which only the Father and the angels witnessed, and the one He suffered on the cross in the face of men. These two agonies of Christ are the boundaries of my destiny. I come and go from one to the other; I leave the trunk of the olive tree only to kiss the tree which is covered with blood. Jesus does not expect, does not require this overwhelming vigilance from every creature, nor even from a large number. Every vocation is unique; I am not an example for the band."

Nothing is more anti-Christian than that maxim to which, centuries after Margaret, men were to adhere: "Act in such a way that your action may serve universal law." There is nothing more specific than the way which has been assigned to us, though we are all bound to imitate Christ. But Jesus carries all vocations within Himself since He has suffered all expiations. Everyone follows his own route, everyone bears his own burden, and they are a route and a burden distinct from all others; and yet all are fused in the same cross of the Lord; these countless individual pathways end in the same agony, the same death, the same resurrection.

The sentryship of the poor penitent of Cor-

tona who has been asleep for seven centuries
and who today would pass for a lunatic has
been taken up anew from year to year; to-day
another person in some cloister or someone lost
in the throng has inherited the same password.
We see her, this Margaret of Cortona, crouch-
ing behind a pillar of our parish church and
we do not recognize her.

CHAPTER XXVIII

God's Words or the Demon's

DESPITE THIS FEAR WHICH SHE NEVER CEASED to feel, though it was the demon and not the Lord who was speaking to her, did she not, in fact, sometimes take a suggestion from the darkness for a statement of the Lord? Any one of them which Brother Giunta tells us about might cast doubts on its origin. After the most tender prayer, in which Margaret begged the divine flame "never to grow cool," she received a strange reproach: "Margaret, you think only of yourself."

A strange reproach; for the saintly daughter, born in the dawn of Franciscan charity, practiced it to the point of folly. It was not enough for her, in Pascal's words, "in wretchedness, to serve the wretched"; for she tore herself away from contemplation in order to

establish and maintain what to-day is called
"works." She was the founder of hospitals, of
the House of Mercy at Cortona which seems
to have been the first big hospital in Italy. In
1286 she organized the corporation of our
Lady of Mercy for serving sick people. She
grouped under the name of *Poverelle* some
young women of the Third Order. Like most
of the great ecstatic saints, she achieved the
miracle of a passionate contemplation of God
during every second of a life consumed by
active charity.

She was even obliged to mingle in the politics of Cortona. This was not what Margaret
was dreaming of when, with Brother Giunta
as intermediary, she forced herself to reconcile
warring factions, to disarm the anger of certain great families, such as the Rossis or the
Rechabenis. The humble penitent also had to
deal with the bishop of Arezzo, the head of an
army before which Cortona trembled, whom
she had first to placate and who ended misera-
bly on the field of battle. The Emperor, the
Pope, the King of Sicily seem, if not to have
accepted her arbitration, at least to have re-

ceived her advice with respect. She had to take
part in Franciscan quarrels. . . . "You think
only of yourself!" And yet "others" consumed
her life.

The truth is that the poor daughter thought
only of her God. The only conceivable politics
for her was the crusade, the deliverance of the
Holy Tomb; it was always God. To reach Him
it was quite necessary for her to go through
with her own particular history, her guilty
youth, her humiliations, her penance. She
sought herself in Him only that she might be
engulfed there. She hated herself with a fierce
hate and took pleasure in fleeing from herself,
in consuming herself in that devouring fire to
which the author of the Epistle to the Hebrews
compares our God. It is remarkable that, contrary to her usual practice, the baffled saint
made no reply to this reproach of Jesus.

But how this statement, which is astonishing coming from the lips of Jesus, changes its
significance if we imagine that it was the old
adversary who whispered it in Margaret's ear!
"You think only of yourself . . ." Satan will
never be done with putting all saintliness to the

test on this theme. "Poor ephemeral creatures, what importance you give yourselves!" he repeats endlessly to those seeking perfection. "What a price you attach to your slightest gestures, your slightest thoughts! No pride has ever equalled yours! You make your body and soul the center of creation. You never cease weeping for your sins, as if the fate of humanity were suspended from the reflexes of your flesh. It seems quite natural to you to have the Infinite Being concerned about it, to bother Him as if only He and you existed in the world. You annihilate the world around this illusory tête-à-tête. You surrender yourself, against your own interest, to horrible excesses in order to force God to pay attention to your extravagance. The lowest prostitute is better at self-contempt than you, because she attaches no value to her body. She would not do it the honor of fighting against it or lacerating it; its wretchedness and its shame are enough for her."

Perhaps the eternal liar does not think he is lying when he lets loose in this way. That is just how saints appear to this exile from love,

and that is just how a world for whom Christ
has refused to pray judges them.

As to Margaret, who thought only about
her God, can it be said just as certainly that she
thought only of her neighbor? The truth is that
had she wanted to forget about the others they
would not have allowed her to. From her first
ecstasies to her death, the crowd never stopped
beating against her cell. She assumed until the
end the martyrdom of being unable to dwell
alone with Him she loved. Until the end she
bore others' burdens and not only those of the
sick and poor of the hospital: "One day during
her illness, as she was sitting on a rush mat,
dressed as in winter in a simple tunic which
covered her hair-shirt, she learned from the
Lord that in a village several miles away there
lived a poor and shy man weighed down with
a family, incapable of earning a living, and
without food and clothing. She received an
order to send him this tunic which she had obtained through the charity of others. Immediately she took it off with joy." Brother Bevegnati tells us further: "Our Lord had filled her
with such great charity that crowds came to

her from the farthest points of the neighboring provinces."

And yet the love of her God sometimes inspired her with answers in which human egoism betrayed itself, if not the influence of the Evil One. One day Brother Rinaldo, the brother superior of Arezzo, asked, "Suppose that at this moment, when you are enjoying such great comfort in Christ, a revelation should inform you that a soul loaded with crimes would be condemned to Hell if you did not come to lead it to penance, and that you were given this alternative, either of being deprived of the ineffable joy which you enjoy at this moment and thereby reclaiming this soul by praying for it up to the hour of Tierce, or of letting it remain, in the event that you would not want to be deprived of the sweetness of your comforts, in the state of being condemned to eternal torture. Which would you choose?" Margaret answered, "I tremble to declare myself. If, on the one hand, I renounce my joy in the Lord, I fall into the bitterness of a new death. If, on the other, I abandon this soul, I fear that I should offend the Creator. Therefore, allow me not to reply." How astonishing! She hesitated to give up the pleasure of her colloquy with God for the salvation of a soul. Dared she balance the eternal fate of a soul against an act of contemplation to which it would be easy to return when her mission at the side of the lost creature had been accomplished?

The strangest thing is that the following day the good Shepherd Who gave His life for His sheep and Who left the whole flock to run after one which had strayed approved Margaret's not having answered in this case of conscience put by the superior of Arezzo, and her having hesitated between the salvation of a man and the spiritual delights with which she was filled. Would not this have been the opportunity to make the charge which the Lord once addressed to her: "Do you think only of drinking in My gifts without considering the creatures whom I have redeemed with My blood?"

CHAPTER XXIX

Margaret Before the Host

IT IS SURPRISING THAT IN THE CATHOLIC Church, the most dogmatic of all Christian persuasions, the most hierarchical (and the one which in its theology grants reason so large a place), the mania of the cross throws off all restraint.

It would seem that the personal religion derived from Luther and Calvin should rather have favored experiences of this order. Are there any Margarets of Cortona, Angelas of Foligno, Catherines of Siena, Theresas of Avila, Johns of the Cross, among the Protestants? Is it because they deny the Communion of the Saints, the reversibility of merit? Because the very idea of "merit" is odd to them? Is it because they allow no intercession in their relations with God that their mystics remain in the greatest obscurity?

According to a note in Jean Baruzi's *Saint John of the Cross,* some of the Protestant mystics, such as Poiret, Dutoit, the Count of Fleischbein, Saint Georges of Marsay, would, through the intervention of Madame Guyon, have undergone the influence of Saint John of the Cross. As it is, Protestant faith is very rarely mystical.

However, one could hardly say that the Catholic Church encourages excess in its contemplatives. It prefers rather to be suspicious of it, and, to tell the truth, gives the impression of preferring dead contemplatives to living ones. Everything happens as if the mystic current gains in depth and power by being piped into Roman channels. It would then be incorrect to say with Bergson that official religion is only a vulgarization of the true religion which is mysticism. It would seem rather to be the casing, the matrix; it gives it its form, its lines, keeps it within the confining dam, regularizes its current.

But for the Catholic above all, *God still speaks;* revelation continues through and by means of the church. Whereas for the Protestant everything is forever closed, everything is in the Book so that nothing remains but to interpret, each according to his own inspiration, for us Catholics the adventure with God is continuous; the story is not finished. So little is it finished that Christ is still immolated in the sacrifice of the mass; His blood will flow every morning until the world's last dawn; His living body will be given as food; His forgiveness will absolve sinners as long as there are any on earth.

This is what our Margaret's simple life proves: one of the Catholic dogmas remains in a state of tremendous ferment, and doubtless the essential ferment of this "passional" piety —the dogma which delivers to the contemplative the God he has contemplated, delivers Him entirely, flesh, blood, soul, divinity. By losing faith in the real presence, Calvinism has lost the sense of wonder around which the mystical experience crystallizes. Faith in the real presence, the certainty every morning of holding against one's heart, one's bosom, the Son of man, the Son of God, miraculously abolishes the distance between the creature and the Creator. This abridgment leads the predestined souls directly to ecstasy and union.

This is particularly true of the female saints whose vocation attaches them to Christ's humanity, but it would be more open to discussion in the case of those, both male and female, who, beyond the Second Person, seek the Father and the unfathomable depth of the Trinity. Might it not be said that the mass, the communion of a John of the Cross, was only a point of departure of his ascent, whereas for our Margaret the host remains at the very center of her penance and her joy?

One day, on returning from communion, she cried out, "This morning my soul is greater than the world since it possesses You, You Whom Heaven and Earth do not contain."

The approach of the host threw her into such a state of enchantment that she begged her confessor to give it to her only after the conventual mass because her humility feared to deliver the secret of superhuman joy to those present. Moreover, she kept herself from yielding to the temptation she had to do so. Christ Himself had to order her not to abstain from taking communion on Friday: "Do you not know that My heart has chosen this day to unite itself to the world? Is it not the day when I have pressed humankind to My heart in an embrace, as a father does with his only son?"

The unworthiness of priests overwhelmed her. In an ecstasy she saw one of them washing the Infant God over a chalice and his raised hands were frightfully black. "Mercy!" she cried out, "Mercy! Mercy for those soiled hands." This priest's name was Angiolo; she sent for him and accused him with a violence that, at a later time, she hesitated to use. But she no longer thought herself unworthy of receiving her God. "My Saviour, why do You force me to receive You so often?" One day when she had just taken communion she found herself suddenly in so deep a peace that she could not keep from crying. Jesus asked her whether her soul was fully satisfied; she answered, "The joys I taste at this moment are such that I think that even in Heaven I would still ask for more, so insatiable is my thirst to possess You. Oh, bread of life! Oh, adorable

bread, what energy, what strength do You fill
me with! With what joy You flood Your weak
and wretched servant!" Christ then asked her,
"Then why do you not receive Me every day?"

But this invitation was addressed to the
one and only Margaret. But for secular and
clerical persons who took communion with in-
sufficient purification there were other and
threatening words: "Unhappiness to those
souls!" Margaret heard that curse. "But you,"
He added, "you are My slave because of your
past sins, My servant because of your present
penance, My sister because of your state of
grace, My daughter because of the pledge you
have received of My eternal glory!"

If He urged her daily not to withdraw before the host, in revenge He gave His approval
to a young monk to space his communions
somewhat so that he might not yield to the
tedium produced by habit. The fact is that if
the story of our saint, written by Brother
Giunta Bevegnati, had fallen into the hands of
the great Arnauld and of Pascal, it would
have furnished them with more texts than these

opponents of frequent communion would have needed to strengthen them in their determined opinions.

On this point, as on so many others, the orthodox Christian follows a narrow path, a ridge between two abysses. The author of the *Imitation* said to Christ, "If I live removed from You, I debar myself from life; if I approach it unworthily, I offend You."

Before taking communion the Christian must, therefore, as Saint Paul suggests, put himself to the test; for we are ordered to share in the body of the Lord as often as possible, but dressed in the nuptial robe. And who is ever sure of being dressed in it? How can we be certain that even a sincere confession discharges a past swarming with deeds whose consequences are linked together in spite of us and which still goes on? Our crimes which we believe pardoned continue to infinity to bear fruit. It is understood that the Church pushes little children to the Holy Table not so much because of their present purity (if we had to take Dr. Freud's word for it), as because they have no past, because they do not drag after them the impurities accumulated in the course of life.

But we aging sinners turn about in a circle; to be dressed in the nuptial robe to share in the body of the Lord, but to share also so that that loosely attached robe may not slip from our shoulders. To be pure so that we may take communion; but also to take communion that we may become pure. . . . Yet who knows what excesses we may risk being led into by the rashness of seeing in the Eucharist a remedy for backsliders? The *Provincial Letters* have denounced it furiously. Then what is to be done? Shut your eyes, yield to mercy, in a spirit of confidence pushed to the point of madness; always keep in mind the sentence of Saint Francis of Sales: "The past must be abandoned to God's mercy, the present to our fidelity, the future to divine providence."

All the same, if Margaret of Cortona, consumed, half destroyed by penance, assured— thanks to the inner words and her ecstasy—of being the Lord's beloved, nevertheless shuddered at her own unworthiness before the host, what will sinners say who have been imperfectly washed of their stains and who are always ready to return to the mire? But each Christian life is unique and different; no example is exactly applicable to our particular drama. Mercy embraces the windings of each conscience, takes the form of each misery. "I speak to a God Who knows all," said the author of the *Imitation*, "Who reads within my heart." Our confidence must rest on this divine knowledge—divine, that is, total—of our own history and not on the example of the saints, for then we should risk losing heart.

The saints know no respite. If their ascent is not achieved in one stretch, at least the spiritual zeal which carries them along can not be interrupted for even a single day. Ordinary Christians take advantage of God's silences to take leaves of absence. They deviate a little, they rest in the shade of human tenderness, they seek annihilation near a faithful heart. They imagine that they will be able to resume the way in their own fashion. And it is true that God is the patient tireless One Whom three nails immobilized at the great crossroads; our God is the God Who waits. But the unfaithful

soul who returns to his father has lost the benefit of the first effort. He has to start all over
again. Our spiritual life will have been an uninterrupted succession of false starts. We withdraw when God is silent, that is, at the very
moment when real progress primes the dryness, when sensible devotion no longer dis-
tracts us from Him Whom we seek; we lack
heart at the very entrance to the bare desert of
Faith, while we are finally going to take the
first step toward the unimaginable discovery.

CHAPTER XXX

Margaret's Last Look at Herself and the World

SILENCE COVERS THE LAST NINE YEARS WHICH Margaret lived out in her cell at Sant-Egidio. Brother Giunta was no longer there to collect her words. How can we help thinking that thanks to this separation which God willed, she gathered the really divine, untranslatable words in her heart, those which the good brother no longer spoiled, no longer retouched, no longer fixed with his writing as if he had pinned dead butterflies on cork. She was no longer ordered by him to ask the Lord what He thought of the Franciscans and whether they ought to accept the offer of such and such a chapel; He no longer whispered answers to her in which the Order was exalted above all the other orders.

The amazing thing about the mystical adventure is this gushing forth of love which makes the canalizations of the Church not useless, of course, but invisible. A certain Brother Filippo and a simple priest of the neighboring church of Saint Bagio, Don Badia Ventura, had the power of bringing Christ to Margaret and of forgiving her her errors already a thousand times forgiven. And they disappear in the shadows, and she remains alone with the Creator in the cell, in the hut. Henceforth, no concern about submitting to another that which in its essence is ineffable.

When she reopened her eyes and cast a human glance on the world, she saw at her feet, filling the horizon, the land of her childhood, of her sin, of her guilty passion, of her repentance, of her love. It was given to her to achieve this way of the cross, to which all life leads, with her eyes, without having to stir. Laviano, from which she had been chased, seemed quite close; and that high spot in the distance was Montepulciano where the poor tenderness of her adolescence had taken root, where she had been tormented by the dark hun-

ger which leads the soul infinitely far from
what it desires and ties a whole destiny to the
most changeful thing in the world, the young,
caressing, cruel male. And her eye could make
out the dark line of the woods where he had
been murdered. The fact that Brother Giunta
Bevegnati never mentions his name in his
Legend need not lead us to conclude that she
had cast him from her heart and thought. For
sin creates a relationship between beings which
is not theirs to destroy. It was for this man,
for him first, that she desired to go to the extreme of expiation. For him, in Margaret's eyes
the first of sinners, but also for all of us; it is
we who make necessary the frightful excesses
of the penitent saints. Our own impurity is at
the source of that martyrdom which the true
friends of Christ inflict upon themselves and
which sometimes scandalizes us to the point of
disgust.

Perhaps, then, before this vegetable and
human horizon, where the trees, the stones, the
hidden ways, the black edges of the forests
again came to life beneath her gaze and in her
memory—but, above all, existed eternally in

God—the source and duration of all things
(and it was in Him that she again found them)
—Margaret, half awakened from her ecstasies
and still invaded by her God, took the real
measure of what she called her crime. For
years, from the depths of her penance, her eyes
fixed on the Saviour's cross which she contemplated from below as she crouched on the
ground, she had been strongly impressed by the
infinite price she had to pay for the slightest of
her infidelities. But now, crucified with Christ,
she saw her miseries from the height of the
gibbet. And perhaps she was tempted, not, of
course, to smile at them, but rather to find that
we are limited and weak even in evil, and that
there is an unimaginable disproportion between
our sins and the love which wants to become
incarnate and die for them.

But were her faults as light as they appear
to us? Even if we knew much more about them
than Brother Giunta tells us, we should hardly
know them. The life of a sinner has a face
turned toward the inner life of which she is
the sole witness. The charming disturbances
of youth have their origin in invisible slime.

From the time when we regard the body as the temple of the Holy Ghost, from the time we become aware of the sacred character of that clay where the Trinity reposes, we then understand the mystery of impure sin, impenetrable to those who do not live in the Faith. In *Messe là-bas* Paul Claudel expresses this anguish of the soul which is about to take communion "when it notices that at all moments of its life, the most secret and most dishonorable, it has made the image of the living God participate."

And yet what a temptation for us at certain hours, not to compromise the Infinite with the poor fumbling gestures of instinct. How filled we are with pity for those young lives poisoned by the anguish of relapses, of admissions, by this shame. How easily we can be disarmed by someone "who has not the sense of sin" when he contradicts us on this point.

He is unaware that God reveals Himself only to pure hearts (which is what Rimbaud knew: "Oh, purity! purity! It is this moment of waking which has given me the vision of purity! By the spirit one goes to God! Harrowing misfortune!").

The adversary has never felt that brusque interruption of Grace in us for a single image, a single desire, which our heart has welcomed, has caressed. He has never taken into account the crimes accumulated by those who play with human beings, for whom human beings are playthings.

Yet, we must believe that during the last seven years when Margaret lived far from her confessor and better protected from the curious crowd, she finally resigned herself to her errors which she had so painfully expiated. The memory of them lost their rawness, she put her confidence in Christ that He might love her as she was. Perhaps she even yielded to the pity which, toward the end of his life, Saint Francis of Assisi felt for his poor body, for his "brother the ass." Was Margaret capable of that tenderness which Francis extended even to his tortured flesh? Did there come a day when she no longer made a martyr of herself except out of habit, and another day when her resemblance to the Lord reached such a point that it was no longer necessary to add anything, and nothing more remained to her than to wait for death?

Resemblance to the Son Who was going so far as to unite her with the Father. The Infinite Being permeated this creature whom a pitiless asceticism had stripped of all that was not He. What good was it still to be obstinately bent against flesh which had been made divine by dint of having annihilated itself? Everything was given back to Margaret by a single look. "The great joy of this awakening," writes Saint John of the Cross, "is to know His creatures by God and not God by His creatures."

CHAPTER XXXI

The Caryatids of Grief

SO, IDENTIFIED WITH CHRIST AND, THROUGH
Him, with the Father in the conflagration of
the Spirit, Margaret shared in Their solitude.
In that blessed thirteenth century, Christ was
as lonely as He is to-day, as different from the
world, as foreign to its passions, as incompre-
hensible, and as scandalous. This austere group
above Cortona, of a whipped and crucified man-
God and a woman who joined Him through a
torture patiently undertaken for more than
twenty years, has always awakened the same
reprobation in nature.

In the centuries of faith as in the centuries
devoted to reason and science there was never
more than a very small number of men and
women "following God in the deserts of divinity," in the words of the pseudo Denys. Hardly

had Francis of Assisi shut his eyes when his
disciples fought about the spouse he had left
to them, the holy poverty which many among
them had already repudiated. The germ which
was to infest the mendicant orders to the point
at which their corruption was to be one of the
direct causes of the Lutheran reform was already proliferating.

The visible Church, which, in Margaret's
century, was in charge of teaching and spread-
ing the Gospel, seemed more foreign to his
spirit than it does now. How can one dare speak
of the popes of that time? But did the booted,
fighting Bishop of Arezzo resemble Christ
more than do the pious administrators of today
with their violet sashes? Must one prefer the
condottieri of the centuries of faith to the pious
diplomats of contemporary history?

The struggles between the spiritual and
temporal for possession of the earth, the rival
influences which, from century to century, have
set the great religious orders against each
other, all this creates an immovable base from
which solitary spirits, whom we recognize in
all ages because they have the same fixed gaze

at the cross and keep the same silence, detach themselves. Popes, monks, priests or laymen, young boys, old men, cloistered or active nuns, students, members of the Young Catholic Workers, holy young girls, they all have this common trait, solitude with their God, agony with Him, suffering, death with Him—but also a peace, a joy born of very pure love, repose in the forgetfulness of all things, in the deprivation of all things which are of the world.

If they are associated with the Church, too often they receive from the hierarchy only the barest stipend so that they may resemble their Master as much as possible. There is hardly any life of a monachal saint, of a religious saint, in which there is not found the prison which his superiors contrived for Saint John of the Cross. We know the true story of little Sister Theresa of Lisieux. An inflexible prior, an archbishop who made his priests weep, were given the mission of having those who were entrusted to them advance, if possible, to the transforming union.

What the Holy Church appears to be from the outside, what its establishment in the world makes inevitable, its diplomacy, its immense organization, the material help it receives from the ruling classes throughout the world, would serve no purpose did there not exist, to uphold it between earth and heaven, these caryatids of grief, these saints with lacerated shoulders whom an immense subterranean network of grace unites to one another.

They emerge above the invisible Church Militant; they testify before history to mankind's uninterrupted effort to surpass itself to the point of being divine—an effort made manifest by the same steps in the most humble and the most glorious destinies; at the side of this beggar-woman, the kneeling man taking communion is Blaise Pascal. The inhuman treatment which Margaret of Cortona inflicted upon herself is proportionate to a love which is disproportionate to the point of madness. And yet it is the same love which burns, little as it may be, in the souls of the simple faithful (it is already so beautiful a thing to be entitled to be called faithful!).

Among these simple faithful, hardly a one seeks suffering willingly; it is enough for them to accept the part set aside for them, from the everyday trials, "those masters God gives with His own hand" from the daily dust of boredom and vexations which floats above what Theresa of the Child Jesus called "the little way", to the most brutal blows which lie in wait for us at every turning and which multiply as we tend toward our decline: the sick heart, the already corrupted flesh, the cunning ravages in the secret places of the body—the thing the doctor suddenly tells us on some quite ordinary day— the street noises come in through the open window, a bird sings, and you look this suddenly unmasked death in the face. And even if we are spared this hour, this is the horror in which we must always end, this last desert of agony.

CHAPTER XXXII

The Temptation of Pathos

WHAT IS IT THEN WHICH HOLDS THE SIMPLE believer who does not share the joys of the saint; what binds him to the commandments of the Church? What is it which leads him to kneel automatically in accordance with the ritual? I do not mean to speak of the routinized flock at the noon masses, gathered near the doors and waiting for the thing to be done with. As far as those are concerned, whether it is a matter of childhood reflexes, social conventions, a vague fear of hell, they do not interest us.

But noble souls, far removed from all holiness and having only a very meager faith, persist all the same in a commonplace religious life. The adversary, who attributes the lowest motives to them—the need to be helped, protected, the fear of risk, the desire for compensation in another life—fails to see a cause which it would be easy to draw from mildly pious souls, the taste for dramatizing so flat, so grey an existence, for enriching it within.

There is no creature so out of grace that faith does not involve him in solemn debate with the Increate Being, and whose slightest replies do not resound beyond the spheres. Imperfect though it may be, every inward religion assures each destiny an infinite prolongation. The liturgy orchestrates life, the sacraments keep a fire going, sometimes a weak flame, sometimes a bright, strong one.

The fate of a soul is at stake every second; aye, its eternity occupies a second; it is at the mercy of a lustful look, of a smile which consents, and can at every moment be dashed down: infernal and heavenly game in which man risks the immortal part of his being.

Despite the mechanics of worship, dry sermons, bastardized services, the least important Christian in a state of grace knows that he shelters the Father, the Son, and the Holy Ghost and that They make Their dwelling within him. He has only to shut his eyes for the Pentecostal wind blowing within him to lift up and carry off the poor daily cares as if they were straws.

Every morning the mass bathes the day which starts with an atmosphere of grandeur, isolates it, defends it against the immense vulgarity of men and things. I think of a certain friend whom human poetry and human love no longer content, who no longer even imagines that one can breathe and move outside of that terrifying and tender presence. Perhaps those who lose their faith have never tasted the full sweetness of the Lord. One is never cured of God when one has known Him. Those who reject Him have not possessed Him.

Such is the secret of Christ's victory over certain souls despite His unbelievable demand: "Be you therefore perfect, as also your Heavenly Father is perfect." In their eyes nothing in the world is more delightful than the charm of that adventure which they have launched, than the passionate interest in a drama going on every second, one which will be resolved with their last breath.

How many men, and those among the best, cannot bear life *as it is?* There we have the real human motive for a Christian life—but one which is not enough to get the soul beyond the first step.

As a source of exaltation Christianity is very quickly used up. Whence that brusque withdrawal from God to things, that weariness, then the disgust with liturgy, those backslidings followed by grovelling returns to the confessional; what misery and shame in the Christian life which does not turn to holiness!

However, this is the lot of Christians who, in the religious life, are chiefly seeking spices to whet their taste for life. Nothing of the senses comes from God. We shall have given an infinite price for the quiverings of corrupted nature in contact with the sacred host.

But holiness begins at that point where the satisfactions of the flesh are over, in a state of Grace. Margaret of Cortona bears witness to this, like all her brothers and sisters who lost themselves and found themselves in the unimaginable union.

Margaret does not set up the sublime irregularity of her saintly life, that irrationality of a love which we have difficulty in conceiving, as an example to follow; yet, far as she may precede us, as far ahead of us as she may be hurrying, it is quite certain that we are bound the same way. Almost all of us will die without having reached, nor even approached, the cell where, during her seven last years, she listened to the silence of God, more enriching than any of the words with which she had been intoxicated. That does not keep the cell from standing and waiting for us at the end of the unknown path; but because of our relapses, as we are ceaselessly retrograde, and because we are satisfied with the intermittent pathos which, for us, is what the religious life leads to, we shall never come to it.

Despite this incurable misery, it is not impossible nor forbidden, in comparing Margaret's experience to that of the other great mystics, to recapitulate the stages of the journey we might ourselves have attempted if we had been saints.

CHAPTER XXXIII

The Stages of the Ascent
Toward the Father

AND FIRST OF ALL, TO BEGIN WITH, THE DISGUST we have felt at times at a defeat, a deception, but without lingering over it for long—that disgust with every created thing which, among the saints, is born of a nostalgic love of God. Human love helps us understand this detachment from everything which is not the object of our tender love. All of us, men and women alike, have known a moment of unimaginable drabness when a single creature was absent, a discoloring of the world because it was no longer reflected in the beloved face.

Henceforth Margaret did without formulas in addressing herself to that God Who was the sole object of her quest and her love; her prayer became an inner one; it would no longer have been possible for her then to bother with ideas (whence those sighs, appeals, sobs, those cries which are substitutes for speeches and set prayers). Her sole desire was to live alone with her love. Nothing counted for her any more. There was no other happiness than this rest, this quietness, this intense sleep. Did Margaret's directors realize what was at stake all through the exhausting struggle that she carried on to be allowed to isolate herself in the cell of Mount Sant-Egidio, and that their opposition was as cruel as the refusal of a glass of water to a creature dying of thirst?

But at last, after her hard victory, there she was alone with her love. That intense sleep. To attain it she had to renounce the knowledge of God through the senses. That peace which surpasses all peace prevailed far beyond suspect effusions; it was as if all her inner powers were bound up together; the infinitely idle soul sustained itself beneath the gaze of the Trinity in a kind of motionless flight. Inexpressible happiness, but we had a presentiment of it when Margaret had a relapse, or rather when

she persuaded herself that she had had one.
Desertion by God, apparent desertion—one can
not measure its horror for the soul which has
known the peace "quae exsuperat omnem
sensum." Even when she forced herself to believe, on the faith of her director, that God
penetrates us the more when it seems to us that
we have lost Him forever, even if she meditated
on the words of the *Imitation:* "when you think
you are far from Me, then it is that I am often
nearest," the soul feels that the hand which up
to then had supported it is now failing it, as if
it were suspended and abandoned between two
worlds. Impossible to go back at this stage of
the ascent, for, according to Saint John of the
Cross, "God transfers the properties and the
strength of the senses to the spirit." That is, it
is no longer given to the soul to take root again
in the physical world. Its sources are dried up
and the foods of the earth do not nourish it.
Season of dryness, of aridity, but also of a
supernatural, overwhelming lucidity.

It astonishes us that, after years of fierce
penance, Margaret still hated herself with a
deadly hate for the miseries which she had a

thousand times expiated. At this last turning
her essential blemish appeared to her, a vision
which is inflicted only on the great mystics on
the eve of the transforming union. The shame
of the saints, the disgust they inspire in themselves, is neither forced nor provoked. In the
blaze of the Trinity which they are approaching they see themselves to the very bottom of
their souls—a knowledge the like of which
could not be had by any natural introspection, a
light which does not pardon, a fire which consumed the desert toward which Margaret, intoxicated with lucidity, was advancing. And
she would doubtless have lost heart had she not
been forewarned that the recent consolations
would turn her away from the God Whose
breath was already scorching her.

To reach Him she had to cross one last
desert, dryness, absolute emptiness. Everyone
had left her, beings and The Being—and not
only left her; everything rose up against her
soul, and God Himself treated her like an
enemy; whence to Margaret, so obviously
weighed down and overwhelmed with favors,
came the terror of being no longer loved, the hell

that had been anticipated—the madness of believing in her reprobation.

Did her senses never rebel? We do not know everything. It was quite proper for Brother Giunta Bevegnati to cast a veil over that which appeared to him to be hardly edifying. But whatever the revival of the urgings of the flesh in Margaret might have been, her soul mastered them and was conscious that to the extent that it exhausted itself, God worked from below to recreate it, without its collaboration.

Certain words lead us to think that a sort of duel was then going on in Margaret between the habit of and taste for the inner voice, and this new power of contemplation which, almost unknown to her, was developing within her. She always returned to the crucified Jesus, but she did so only to bound back; the Spirit raised her up to Him of Whom there was no longer a face to haunt her. She was carried off to conceive, adore, and cherish a love without a face. These abrupt changes of altitude, these thundering re-ascents, followed by descents and falls—these above all, weaken not only the body but the spirit of the saint as well.

The most rigorous penance affects the body only, and can do nothing with the essential impurity of the spirit. There is no asceticism for changing man's spirit. Therefore, Grace must corrode the very substance of the creature to whom Increate Love wishes to unite itself. In the little cell above Cortona where, by Christ's order, an altar was set up, a non-human hand succeeded in preparing Margaret. To take Saint Theresa's word for it, even ecstasy then becomes painful. If one may say so, God acts as if He were absent. The soul advances into heaven, but into a deserted heaven; not nothingness, but an absence, an infinite flight—an infinity which disappears.

Here is the last turning of the unknown way where the Creator will insinuate Himself into the destroyed creature like a flood. God surrounds the soul now emptied of all which is not God, invades it, occupies it, and finally possesses it. "I who have been darkness," murmured the dumbfounded Margaret, "I who have been darker than night!" Christ replied, "For love of you, new light, I bless the cell where you live concealed in My love."

Sometimes an angel also spoke to her, and its words confirm us in the notion that she followed the route quite as we have described it. The angel said to her, "You are like a house which has been set on fire; it burns until it is completely consumed; so you remain in tribulation to the very end. Although you have peace, you live in a state of war. Gold is purified in the furnace. . . . God waits for the heart and makes it heedful from the time of love's first desire; and when that love demands Him ardently, He no longer postpones returning to the soul. Love then achieves in a moment what is accomplished only in time in souls of less ardent charity. There are three degrees in this pure love by which the faithful and fervent soul draws its God to itself. When the soul considers itself destitute of all divine charity, nothing can comfort it but God. It is then that the Most High inclines toward and sympathizes with the creature who has been given over to anguish. . . . But before the universal Father of all goes into the soul created and redeemed by Him, love purifies the heart of all its illusions. The third degree of love is a desire which inflames the spirit like fire. In this state the soul does not cease to seek its beloved, its spouse, everywhere and in everything."

Thus, the angel helped Margaret become aware of the road to be traveled and even marked for her the stages of her ascent toward the Father.

CHAPTER XXXIV

Death and Last Ecstasy

WE NOW COME TO THE MONTH OF FEBRUARY IN the year 1297 when Margaret was to enter her rest. The very day and hour (which was that of dawn) were known to her in advance. She waited, her arms paralyzed, her soul already out of her body at certain moments. Brother Giunta Bevegnati had been returned to her or rather, it was she who had been returned to the good brother. The superhuman adventure had been achieved without anyone's help. The union had been accomplished in the creature's secret depths to which the director had no access. No longer anyone in the world but herself and her Creator. No other need but for a consecrated hand to give her the host and to absolve her.

From February sixth to the dawn of the twenty-second, when she passed to eternity, she took no food. That is all we know about her death. A hagiographer would be wasting his time trying to orchestrate so meagre a theme; a fifty-year old woman, consumed for twenty-five years by a fierce penance, dies in a corner of her cell.

The perfume which those who are present at the death of a saint always think they smell floated around her pallet. That is the only fact which Brother Bevegnati has retained and established. He also tells that at the same hour a contemplative at Citta di Castillo saw Margaret enter Heaven amidst a tumult of souls which she had delivered, and she avouched that the woman of Cortona was Christ's new Magdalene. Did Margaret say at this moment, as is reported in her various *Lives,* "The way of salvation is easy; it is enough to love?" Did she have sacred texts read to her by Brother Giunta? Were her old friends present, the Moscari women in particular? Her biographers affirm this with no proof, since Brother Giunta says nothing about the matter.

Nor does he tell us that the unfortunate child was at his mother's bedside. It does no

good to be the son of a saint, at least in this
world, if one has not become a saint himself.
One can picture a man, a monk, the child of this
ecstatic woman's sin, his revolts which made
him feel ashamed, the exasperated veneration
he gave to the gently implacable creature of
whom he had been born. Perhaps he drove off
this sacrilegious thought: "As for her, she had
her season of joy on earth, a hot and full youth,
while I . . ." But perhaps she drew him after
her along the unknown route, and, as an ardent
monk, he envied his mother's reaching the end
of the exhausting earthly journey.

The death of a saint who is already in God
is only the confirmation of a state of actuality.
The poor body which she dragged along the
unknown way is finally detached. How could it
have held on so far? She abandoned it to the
civil and religious authorities, to the Franciscans, to the crowd. Here was that cast-off carcass which she had hated so much now being
perfumed with incense and surrounded with
aromatics. The iron coffin was sealed up in the
Sant-Egidio oratory which Margaret had re-
stored. It goes without saying that miracles oc-

curred thick and fast. But the greatest of all remains that of her saintliness, what Love accomplished in a lost girl.

A girl who had been lost. That is what we must always return to when the torture she inflicted upon herself irritates or disturbs our reason. The rigorous penance of the Franciscan saint who preceded her in glory, Clara of Assisi (who died in 1253 when Margaret was still only a little girl) never had the character of a hatred and, as it were, a vengeance with which the soul seeks to satiate itself at the body's expense. Clara passed from the purest childhood to holy poverty and contemplation. Her passion for total destitution, inherited from her father Francis, was the fruit of the love she had vowed to the child of the manger. But she warned her daughters against the excesses with which Margaret later intoxicated herself. "Our body is not made of iron," Clara wrote to her beloved Agnes of Bohemia. "Our strength is not that of stone. . . . Live and hope in the Lord, and let your service be according to reason. Modify your holocaust with the salt of prudence."

If Margaret had received such a message, she would perhaps have replied to Clara, "You know not what a memory the flesh keeps of crimes which have been a thousand times expiated, what germs proliferate in a body which once consented to mortal love; you who have returned your child's heart to God just as you received it do not know this."

There can be no doubt that in that dawn of February 22nd, 1297, she had passed beyond, surmounted that madness of expiation. We do not know what Margaret said to herself on the threshold of eternity. Its echo has not come down to us as has that which we still hear around the death-bed of the dying Saint Clara, those tender and sublime appeasements with which the poor woman of Assisi comforted her soul: "Go in all peace, because you have a good guide to show you the way; depart without fear, for He who created you has sanctified and loves you with a tender love as a mother loves her only son. Be blessed, oh My God Who created me, be blessed eternally." We believe that the same confidence, the same certainty supported the penitent of Cortona in her agony,

"Do you see," Clara of Assisi asked a sister a short while before dying, "my sweet child, do you see the King of Glory as I see Him?"

Margaret, too, saw the King of Glory. And the King of Glory looked at her with that tender brooding look which only the contemplative souls have known and which we, the simple faithful, shall never know, because of that harsh law which Tauler has stated: "To aspire to the double enjoyment of God and His creatures, though you weep for it with blood, it can not be."

The thing that distinguishes us ordinary Christians is that we have a daily, unexceptionable experience of the truth stated by Tauler. We know that the Beloved waits for us beyond things, beyond creatures. But we have not the strength to leap over that living barrier. Let us learn, therefore, not to dread death, but even to cherish it—death, which discards things and creatures, finally unmasks God and delivers us to Him.

There is nothing more comforting than the remark of Saint Theresa "that there is a great resemblance between ecstasy and death."

Death, the only ecstasy which will be given to us poor Christians to know.

For Margaret agony was a prolonged ecstasy, death an accomplished ecstasy. For years flesh and blood had barely had any part in her union with God; she attained it less and less through the senses. Her half submerged soul remained completely exposed to the flood which was to break over her when once the dam of the body would be broken.

But however far she might have gone beyond the human God, nevertheless the Son of man, at whose side she had been during His passion, throughout a penance of so many years, had to be there to help her in the passage; and one last time on earth she contemplated that face, no longer covered with spit, but triumphant, radiant, as it appeared to Stephen, the first martyr: *"Here do I see the open heavens and the Son of man seated at the right hand side of God."*

Margaret of Cortona might have been a different saint, though just as strictly bound to God, if the Christ of Glory, the conqueror of the world and of death, had dominated her life, and not the sacrificed Lamb, the Man of Sorrows.

The truth may be, perhaps, that it was neither the King of Glory nor the victim crowned with thorns who received her last look. Perhaps, at the approach of death, when the half detached soul floated at the very threshold of eternity, she saw the Lord as He actually was, wandering at the border of Heaven and earth along the way to Emaus, as Rembrandt has painted Him, "pale, emaciated, with blackish lips, where the torture had left its mark." But what do we know about the death of the saints? Is there a single one of them who, in his last hour, has not uttered the unimaginable cry of the dying Son, "My God, My God, why hast thou forsaken me?" Perhaps Margaret grew faint before this last ordeal and shut her eyes so that she might not see the infinite void.

CHAPTER XXXV

Temptation Before a Corpse

AND NOW SHALL I LISTEN TO WHAT THE ADVER-
sary whispers to me because he suffers to see me
on my knees before my dead heroine? "The perfume emanating from this body does not console us," he says, "nor do the miracles around
it. Now is the time that this mouth should suddenly have spoken. But the corpse of a saint
keeps the secret of all saints. It enters the great
common silence. What more are we to expect
from that carcass which has descended from a
cross than from a body consumed by debauchery? Both of them are motionless, both of them
are dumb, forever. It has been written of living
mystics that they are the explorers and witnesses of an invisible world. In order to believe
that they have returned from it, we would
first have to assure ourselves that they have

penetrated it, and doubtless they attest that they have seen, touched, and possessed the face-less Love. And it is true that they have fallen to the ground with ecstasy before the mob. They quiver beneath a claw that is not seen. But it is precisely this claw that it matters for us to see. We shall never know whether they are at once victims and dupes of their heart which is di-vided in two, which is torn, to attain the cruel, the delicious increase of ecstasy."

Thus speaks the adversary. And it is true that the death of the saints puts up the same inexorable wall in front of us as does every other death. We hit our heads against the same stone wall. Kept intact like those of Saint Clara of Assisi or Saint Charles Borromée, their mummified bodies offer us only a lesson of nothingness. And yet every generation, like the one which saw the Son of Man live and die, asks for signs. The mystics hold us only because of the promise that they will make us touch the substance of what we hope for. . . . And then they die and nothing remains of them but some words prudently touched up by their confessor.

But what of it! Have not the greatest of

them learned that it is God's will that we must believe in Him in the dark? "Blessed are they that have not seen and have believed." We ought not expect from the saints a proof which would exempt us from believing. On the contrary, they teach us to believe without comfort and without proof—to give everything in advance in exchange for a treasure which is not seen, for a priceless pearl, but one which is at the bottom of an ocean from which no diver has ever returned.

The legend of their life, the dialogues of fire of a Margaret of Cortona, an Angela of Foligno, a Catherine of Siena, the Canticle of Saint John of the Cross, which we travelers on earth are enchanted with keep us from being afraid in the dark; they help us walk in the night without losing heart. I open my prayer-book to the Saturday page of Holy Week where the Litanies of the Saints are found, and from the depths of my darkness, I call you by your names one by one; I raise up your innumerable, silent, but eternally living army, confessors, virgins, penitents, apostles, martyrs—jubilant cortege of the lamb.

CHAPTER XXXVI

Examination of Conscience

I AM ASHAMED OF HAVING IN THE COURSE OF this story constantly begged indulgence toward Saint Margaret's excesses. Yet, in this horrible world of 1943 when the torture that mankind inflicts upon itself exceeds all measure, it would be strange for the reader of this Life to dare to express disgust.

For the world hates itself infinitely more than Margaret hated herself. The desire for power devotes itself to tearing its heart apart, not in a crisis of mad fury, but slowly, year by year; and it is not too much for all the genius of inventors, all the heroism of the young men, all the patience of the poor in the whole world, to lead this immense collective martyrdom to its perfection. One may refuse to go into the reasons for that love but not to be astonished that she who loved followed in the footsteps of her Beloved and complied with Him strictly.

Perhaps it is a mistake to persuade one's self that suffering is a cash payment for crime, yet that has been believed since there have been men; and even those who live without God act in practice as if they believed it. It is a matter of everyday language to say of a condemned man that he has paid his debt. Margaret was not unreasonable in having believed that she too had contracted a debt during her delicious and criminal youth and in having forced herself to discharge it to the last penny.

It is true that her faith went further. She had no doubt about the redeeming power of her penance and that every one of us may, if he wishes, cooperate in the Passion of Christ. Though she might have been mistaken on this point with the whole Catholic Church, the torture she inflicted upon herself would have been an error of love, but, all the same, a testimony of love. Let the man of 1943 whose fate it is to hate and be hated, to destroy and be destroyed, look twice before scoffing and shrugging his shoulders; let him heed the secret of this holy

madness. At bottom, nothing which comes from
love is horrible. We do not have to feel sorry
for those who love because of the harm they
do themselves. In this universe of terror where
the will to power puts mechanized men on the
rampage and where *God is dead,* if we are to
believe Zarathustra, what is left here below
that this creature who is both murderer and
victim can love? Nothing else but what the very
philosopher of the *Will to Power* proposed to
himself as the last consolation: *amor fati;* according to Nietzsche it remains for man to love
his horrible destiny.

Wondrous madness of Margaret which
overthrows the idol, which smashes the iron
collar! Well, yes, there she was free to shave
her head, to deprive herself of food, to besmear
her face, to seem to abandon her little boy—
beyond all reason? Let the cross be a madness,
let the truth be mad, that stupefying affirma-
tion of Saint Paul, I shall not have truly understood it, I shall finally have entered it only at
this turning point of history, only during that
interval of time in which we are condemned to
suffer.

For two thousand years, from Socrates to Hegel and Marx, the wisest men have sought and thought they found what was proper for right living and for regulating the relationships of men, between individuals, nations, and social classes. They have extracted the laws of history which determine the human condition. They know how to act to assure the definitive victory of reason and the mastery of man over things. Others go back to the old disciplines and re-establish in society the hierarchies they deem necessary for man. What methods! What appropriate techniques for these methods!

Every great nation has in its turn aspired to have the rest of the world benefit by its wisdom. It has striven to do so by sword and fire, first to convince its own citizens, then beyond its borders as far as its force could avail. Chemists and physicists, masters of matter, have placed their best arguments in the service of antagonistic ideologies. A two thousand pound bomb has the same persuasive power regardless of the colors of the plane which drops it.

The world submissive to reason is also a world submissive to morality—morality being a matter of reason. Evidently it deems that Margaret would have done better by working to bring up her little boy; pretty as she was, she would doubtless have found a decent man to marry her and would have given other children to her country.

The strange thing is that it has been a mission of the religion which our penitent was concerned with, the Holy Church itself, to make this truth reasonable. In this it has succeeded to the point of earning the praises of thoughtful men and the admiration of political philosophers. Theologians find a satisfactory answer to all questions. What was the tree of the knowledge of good and evil? How reconcile God's freedom and man's freedom?

What does original sin consist of? How resolve the problem of evil? Why does the fault of the first couple weigh on the whole human race? Why has not the incarnation of the Son of God closed the gates of Hell forever? How does Christ give His body to be eaten and His blood to be drunk? It is surely not impossible for logicians to make all these matters accept-

able to an intelligent mind. There is no lack of
Christians, and those among the best, whom
Saint Thomas Aquinas has convinced and who,
with the help of grace, have found faith at the
end of a syllogism.

But in the last analysis, we must always go
back to the little book full of absurd sayings
(according to human reason) and stories both
delightful and revolting. Is it wise to be un-
occupied with either food or clothing? Is lack
of foresight a virtue? Why is the prodigal son
always treated better than the older brother
who has always been faithful? Why are not the
workmen who have borne the whole weight and
heat of the day paid more than the lazy and
clever who come to the yard at the last hour
when the heat has dropped? Why is the lazy
Mary preferred to Martha? Is it good to bring
war and not peace? To separate husband from
wife and brother from brother? All the com-
mentaries vainly strive to soften the meaning
of so outrageously clear a lesson. It is clear
that God's justice scoffs at our justice, that the
laws of the Kingdom of God scoff at those of

the sons of Adam—of that Adam who gathered from the tree of the knowledge of good and evil the fruit whose poison still burns us.

But, believers or unbelievers, we feel strongly that the whole power and enchantment of the Gospel reside in the scandal it stirs up; the more our reason protests, the more we are enchanted. Yet, suppose truth did not conform to reason or human logic; suppose it were really the madness which Saint Paul denounced, and Tertullian after him—that *absurdity;* suppose it wandered veiled among men, as Pascal puts it, and had to be seized by a method unknown to Descartes and all thinkers after him; suppose, in this universe ruled by the laws of reason and still submissive to the truth of Aristotle, the saints who pass for madmen were found to be the real sages; suppose the true church were recognized less by the letter of its doctrine, however sublime and satisfying to the intelligence it may be, than by the fruit it bears and because it is the Church of saints?

For philosophers only the logical, immaterial, eternal truths are real. But for each one of us the real is his self, his hard human condition—precisely what for the stoic sages, our masters, is unimportant and doesn't count. They scoff at our individual life, providing we know how to harden ourselves against it and remain faithful, whatever happens, to the laws of reason and the principles of reasonable morality.

Only there has been nothing they can do about the fact that there has not been less docility among us since Someone came and uttered certain illogical and highly absurd words. A restlessness has been born, a desire to seek by methods other than those of the masters a truth different from theirs, a truth which concerns our personal life, our conscience, our most secret drama.

Such is the law of our nature. Despite her extravagances Margaret of Cortona obeyed her law which was to pursue a more abstract truth, but one incarnate for her, for love of her. Margaret behaved as though there were only she and God in the world. But when she, or any other great mystic, speaks of this madness we are millions of miles away from knowing what she is talking about.

No, indeed, we do not have to choose between the God of the philosophers and the savants, the author of geometric truths and the God Who besieges us from within (for He has established His dwelling in our soul) and from without (for the Word was made flesh and we have received testimony from those whose eyes have seen Him, whose hands have touched Him). It is no longer important for us to know whether the abstract God, the prime mover of Descartes, is more conformable to healthy reason than the God Who loves His creature, Who grants or refuses him grace— for we have believed in a single thing, but one which conforms to the demand of our soul and which suffices for our joy: it is that God is love. We have taken "certain obscure Jews," disciples of a crucified man, at their word, and John, the first of all: "That which was from the beginning, which we have heard, which we have seen with our eyes, which we have looked upon and our hands have handled, of the word of life . . . we declare unto you that you also may have fellowship with us. . . . We know that we have passed from death to life, because we love the brethren. . . . In this we have known the charity of God, because he hath laid down his life for us: and we ought to lay down our lives for the brethren. . . . My little children, let us not love in word nor in tongue, but in deed and in truth. . . . For if our heart reprehend us, God is greater than our heart."

We have believed in this madness, the insertion of eternity in time, of God in ephemeral man. We have believed the unbelievable, that the Infinite Being was engulfed in poor human history.

And doubtless if Margaret of Cortona believed in that love to the point of sacrificing her life for it day after day, it was because she had received a sign, and because, before all the inner utterances with which she was favored, she had listened to one, less distinct perhaps, but just as imperious, before the corpse of her lover and, a little later, beneath the fig-tree in her father's garden. The intermittent fidelity of the last of the faithful is no longer explicable by any reasoning he might have carried on, by a decision maturely reflected upon, but because Someone touched him to the heart, because there is a source of tears within him which has once gushed forth and which will not dry up again. "It is not you who have chosen Me; it is I who have chosen you," said the Lord. Such is the mystery of grace in its unfathomable simplicity.

A short time before Margaret came into the world, Pope Gregory the Ninth, fulminating against Emperor Frederick the Second, accused him of maintaining "that one should believe absolutely only what is proved by the law of things and by natural reason." If someone had asked the humble Margaret this question and if she had been able to understand its import she would doubtless have protested that she trusted natural reason in everything that concerns the body and not only in scientific and philosophical research, but in theology as well. She would only have been demanding the right to believe that there exists an order of charity, which Pascal tells us about in a well-known fragment, that it is infinitely higher than that of the body and that of the spirit, and has its own mode of investigation and knowledge, its proofs, its knowledge of the heart which reason does not know.

What good is it to deny that on the plane of reason and from the point of view of Kantian morality, Margaret of Cortona is indefensible? It is also true that the Church appeals to human reason by its theology and satisfies it. It does not keep it from defying this same reason in raising a Margaret of Cortona or a Benoit Labre on the altars. Despite its Hellenic tradition and everything it has borrowed from Aristotle, the Church, because it is of God, cannot help defying human reason. She is, if I dare say so, stronger than it is. The Church of scholasticism kneels before the sublime madmen of the Cross, and thereby we recognize that it is the true Church, the Church of Jesus Christ, the Church of the Virgin, the Church of the Saints.